About the author

SIMONE SEKERS has been a regular columnist with the *Daily Telegraph* and the *Sunday Telegraph* for some years, as well as contributing to a number of books and magazines.

She has always believed in the advantages of a well-stocked store-cupboard to add interest and variety to everyday cooking, and that a few minutes spent prolonging the life of seasonal food pays dividends in terms of time and money later in the year.

As her passion for cooking is only equalled by her passion for gardening, and reading old cookery books, almost all her own books combine these elements. Among them are *Effortless Entertaining* (Piatkus), *Fine Foods* (Hodder and Stoughton) and *The National Trust Book of Fruit and Vegetable Cookery*.

BBC BOOKS' QUICK & EASY COOKERY SERIES

Launched in 1989 by Ken Hom and Sarah Brown, the *Quick & Easy Cookery* series is a culinary winner. Everything about the titles is aimed at quick and easy recipes – the ingredients, the cooking methods and the menu section at the back of the books. Eight pages of colour photographs are also included to provide a flash of inspiration for the frantic or faint-hearted.

SIMONE SEKERS'
QUICK & EASY
PRESERVES

BBC BOOKS

To all the friends and family, especially my husband,
who tried and tested these recipes with such great gusto

Published by BBC Books,
a division of BBC Enterprises Limited,
Woodlands, 80 Wood Lane
London W12 0TT

First published 1994
Copyright © Simone Sekers 1994
The moral right of the author has been asserted
ISBN 0 563 36946 9

BBC Quick & Easy
is a trademark of the
British Broadcasting Corporation

Designed by Peter Bridgewater
Photographs by Philip Webb
Styling by Philip Webb
Home Economist: Sarah Ramsbottom

Set in Bembo by Create Publishing Services Ltd, Bath

Printed and bound in Great Britain by Clays Ltd, St Ives Plc
Colour separation by Technik Ltd, Berkhamsted
Colour sections printed by Lawrence Allen Ltd,
Weston-super-Mare
Cover printed by Clays Ltd, St Ives Plc

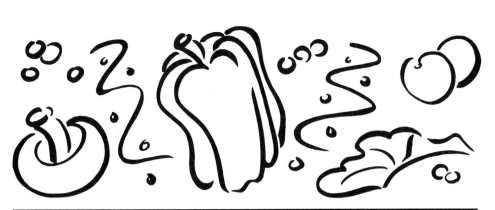

Contents

INTRODUCTION 7

NOTE ON THE RECIPES 8

PRESERVING TIPS AND TECHNIQUES 9

NOTES ON SAFETY 11

USEFUL EQUIPMENT 12

STORE-CUPBOARD INGREDIENTS 15

SAVOURY PRESERVES 19

SWEET PRESERVES 49

POTTING AND CURING 79

FLAVOURINGS, SEASONINGS AND SAUCES 94

CORDIALS, SYRUPS AND LIQUEURS 120

INDEX 133

POSTAL SUPPLIERS 136

INTRODUCTION

Although quick and easy preserves might seem a contradiction in terms, so lengthy and time-consuming does the whole traditional process of preserving food for long-term storage appear, in fact there are lots of ways of producing food for the store-cupboard which involve only minutes of your time. And they can be minutes well spent, since a few spoonfuls of herb-flavoured oil or vinegar, a glass of home-made fruit liqueur or a jar of fruit in syrup will not only make all the difference to meals throughout the year – adding the summery taste of basil in December, for instance – but they make excellent presents as well.

So in this book I give recipes that demonstrate you can make a delicious jam in less than quarter of an hour, spice beef or cure salmon with far less effort (and expense) than going out and buying it, or create your own Mediterranean antipasti at the flourish of a garlic press. The only thing you might need is patience, while the preserve is allowed to mature a little on the shelf. No special equipment is needed; you can always improvize a meat-press with a cake tin, a plate and a jam jar of water, although I do give some ideas for pieces of gadgetry you might consider buying. I have also used ingredients which are widely available, as there is nothing quick and easy about a recipe which calls for rare and peculiar substances.

There are notes on how to avoid giving your family food poisoning, and on which ingredients it is useful to have to hand so that you can take advantage of cheap seasonal produce, together with some addresses of postal suppliers of such things as spices, or lids for jam jars (see page 136).

For each recipe I have given suggested uses for the finished product, and sometimes its by-products too – such as using the sweet-and-sour vinegar from a jar of spiced pears as the basis for a vinaigrette, or the oil from an antipasto as a marinade for grilled fish. Even jams can appear more often than on a slice of bread. Versatility is the most useful talent that a preserve can have, as it is that which will, quickly and easily, give the most mundane meal just that extra bit of zest and originality.

N OTES ON R ECIPES

M ost of us have a hoard of old jam jars we recycle for preserves, and since it is important to have clean, dry and warmed jars ready and waiting for their cargo of jam or chutney, I have given the number of jars required at the beginning of each recipe, based on the following size guidelines:

Any jar well over 454 g (approx. 1 lb) in capacity and up to about 850 g (approx. 2 lb) constitutes a **large** jar – recommended for pickles, fruit in alcohol or syrup and so on.

Any jar between 225 g (8 oz) and 454 g (1 lb) constitutes a **medium** jar – the most useful and easily found size for jams and chutneys.

Any jar 225 g (8 oz) or less in capacity is a **small** jar – a very useful size for presents and the size most often found filled with 'souvenir' jams in the gift shops of stately homes.

For bottle sizes (used for cordials, syrups, liqueurs and sauces), I used the following guidelines:

Large are those which hold about 750 ml (1 ¼ pints) – the average wine bottle size and best for cordials and liqueurs.

Medium are those which hold about 350 ml (12 fl oz) – a good size for vinegars.

Small are those which hold about 250 ml (8 fl oz) – a good size for flavoured oils.

It's a good idea to prepare one extra jar or bottle to be on the safe side.

If a jar or bottle still has a faint smell of its original contents (mustard, or coffee), fill it with lukewarm water and add a generous teaspoonful of bicarbonate of soda. Leave overnight then rinse well, dry and use.

Use either metric or imperial measurements, but don't mix the two.

PRESERVING TIPS AND TECHNIQUES

PECTIN

This is the magic word in jam-making, as it is the element which makes the mixture of fruit and sugar a set jam or jelly rather than a syrup. Some fruit contains less pectin than others, and it is to those that extra pectin sometimes has to be added, either by combining low-pectin fruits with higher pectin ones, or by adding acid in some form, usually lemon juice, or extra pectin on its own. For quick and easy jam-making, sugar-with-pectin (see 'Sugar' on p. 17) is a boon. Fruits naturally high in pectin, which need no extra help, are apples, black- and redcurrants, damsons and gooseberries. Those lowest in pectin include blackberries, cherries, strawberries, rhubarb and rowan berries (see p. 48). The pectin contents of all fruit lessens with the ripening process so use slightly under-ripe, or a mixture of ripe and unripe. Frozen fruit also has a lowered pectin content, so allow for this.

DISSOLVING THE SUGAR

This should be done with care, as it can catch and burn if the heat is too high before all the sugar has dissolved. Even then it isn't an unmitigated disaster – I've made some richly flavoured jams in which the flavour of caramelized sugar undoubtedly played a part – but badly burnt sugar does taste very bitter. Melt the sugar with the liquid and fruit over a low-to-medium heat, stirring frequently until you can no longer feel the grittiness of the sugar under your spoon, then raise the heat to bring the jam to a full rolling boil.

FULL ROLLING BOIL

Another magic jam-making phrase. This is a vigorous bubbling which doesn't disperse and disappear when you stir the jam. Timing the jam to setting point starts when the steady simmer (which can be stirred away) changes to this.

TESTING FOR SETTING POINT

Just drop a little of the jam on to a cold saucer, then see if the surface will wrinkle when you push it gently with your finger. Draw the pan off the heat while you test it, returning it to the heat if the jam on the saucer remains liquid and unwrinkled.

STANDING

If the jam contains discernable bits of fruit, such as the Strawberry and redcurrant preserve on p. 76 or the Rhubarb, orange and ginger jam on p. 77, allow it to stand for about 15 minutes in order to let the jam cool and begin to set. Then stir the jam to distribute the bits of fruit before potting. This simple precaution means that the fruit will stay suspended throughout the jar, rather than bob to the surface as its sets.

WARMING THE JARS

To make sure the glass doesn't crack when you pour in the hot jam, jars must be warmed first. Warming them also drives out any moisture, as the jars must also be absolutely dry. It's best to arrange the jars, without their lids, in the oven on its lowest setting, before you begin the jam-making.

STORAGE

Jams and jellies are best stored in a cool, dry place. This can be difficult in modern kitchens without larders as, while they are dry, they are not always cool. A well-ventilated garage or outhouse is a good alternative. In several of the recipes I also suggest that, once started, a jar should be kept in the fridge.

NOTES ON SAFETY

Preserving is safe if you take certain basic common-sense measures:

1 Transfer the food from the container in which it was cooked to a storage container, and make sure the jar or dish or bowl which you are going to use for storage is thoroughly clean and dry. If in doubt, rinse it out with boiling water and dry it on a clean tea-towel. Use sterilizing fluid for containers for non-alcoholic cordials, as bottles are more difficult to clean thoroughly.

2 Drain cooked meat or fish of its cooking juices before sealing it under a layer of fat or oil.

3 Store potted meat or fish, covered, at a temperature of 5°C or below, in the fridge, but remove to room temperature for about 30 minutes before serving. Provided the food is still covered, this presents no dangers and will make sure that you get the full flavour of the dish; it also makes the food more digestible, as very cold food is very tough on the digestion.

4 Label and date your preserves, be they chutney or potted cheese, and rotate your stock, so that you can check and use them within their safe life-span.

5 Cool and dry storage is important. Damp can cause fermentation, which is why it is so necessary for containers to be dry before filling. Storing oil-preserved foods in too warm an atmosphere will make the oil turn rancid, and will make the vinegar in vinegar-preserved foods evaporate, leaving the top layers high and dry.

6 Best of all, make preserves in relatively small quantities, so that they do get eaten when they are at their best. As children we rather enjoyed 'fizzy' jam, probably because of its mild alcoholic content, but mouldy jam is horrible.

USEFUL EQUIPMENT

F ew of the recipes in this book need any specialist equipment, but there are one or two items which I find particularly useful.

PRESERVING PAN

Because this book concentrates on making small and manageable quantities, a preserving pan isn't strictly necessary if you have a saucepan which will hold about 4 litres (7 pints) comfortably. However, the sloping sides of a traditional preserving pan offer a reduced area nearest the source of heat to lessen the risk of the jam or chutney catching on the bottom, and a greater area at the top to help evaporation of liquid. I invested in a stainless steel pan which holds 8 litres (14 pints), partly because it had a 20 cm (8 inch) diameter base which fits nicely on to the average hotplate cooking area, and partly because it is recognized that the action of acid on aluminium isn't always healthy. But much cheaper and equally good are aluminium pans with non-stick linings, if you don't mind a larger base area of about 25 cm (10 inches). Whatever type you choose, it should have a side handle to help move it safely when full of hot jam.

PRESSURE COOKER

A long-time admirer of the pressure cooker, I find it far quicker to use than the microwave when pre-cooking fruit, such as citrus fruit, for jams and marmalades. It has so many uses in the kitchen and is so efficient at saving fuel, that I think it worth consideration. There are lots of models on the market and many have safety features which should soothe those who are nervous (unnecessarily so) of using this wonderfully useful gadget.

FOOD MILL

Most of us wouldn't be without a food processor or blender these days, but I wouldn't be without my food mill either. It has the great advantage of sieving as well as puréeing – ideal for making plum preserves.

JELLY BAG AND STAND

Having had unhappy and messy experiences rigging up unsafe constructions to strain jellies (one chair up-ended on top of another, a gyrating pillowcase of hot fruit spattering the larder walls puce), I now erect a neat little arrangement of plastic-coated wire into a sturdy frame which comes with its own windsock-shaped nylon straining bag. The frame packs flat when not being used and the bag can go in the washing-machine. The £10 or so that it cost was well worth it.

SPICE BALL

While working on this book I found these small hinged stainless-steel mesh balls excellent for holding spices for flavouring vinegars and pickles. It's much easier than tying them into little squares of muslin with the extra advantage that they hook on to the side of the saucepan and are far easier to fish out. You can use a tea infuser to get the same effect.

COFFEE FILTER

Using a cheap plastic coffee filter and disposable filter papers is the best way of straining vinegars, liqueurs, cordials and flavoured oils, although you can use a muslin-lined sieve as an alternative.

JARS AND BOTTLES

Most of us have a cache of jars and bottles kept for jam-making; it is important to see that they are inspected for spiders and dust, thoroughly washed (although not necessarily sterilized) and dried, and then warmed before having hot jam or chutney poured into them. You can buy new jars if necessary (see page 136 for address of supplier). For the recipes in this book, preserving jars are not strictly necessary. You can use any wide-mouthed jar with a good lid instead. Decorative bottles made of Spanish recycled glass can be bought from kitchen shops and transform the presentation of home-made liqueurs.

LIDS

Although clear cellophane lids and waxed circles are traditional for jam-making, I think most people prefer to use more durable lids. Always keep the lid with the jar, so that there are no last-minute scrambles for the right lid – it also keeps the jar cleaner in storage too. Again, you can buy twist-off lids to match the jars mentioned above and these are plastic-lined to make them safe to use with vinegar–based preserves; vinegar corrodes metal, so if you do have to use an unlined metal lid, cap the jar or bottle with a piece of polythene before screwing on the lid.

JAM FUNNELS

Not essential, but a non-stick funnel is very helpful for directing hot, sticky preserves exactly where you want them to go, without those dribbles down the side of the jar that you have to remember to wipe off before storing.

BRINE CONTAINER

A plastic bucket which holds 4.5 litres (1 gallon) makes a good container for brine (see p. 90), scrub it out with boiling water before and after use, and find a plate which will fit inside it to keep the meat immersed. You will also need a weight, which can't be the ubiquitous can of beans because that would go rusty on contact with the brine and taint it. A jam or preserving jar of water does very well and can be properly cleaned too. It also comes in handy for weighting Spiced beef (see page 88) and Pickled tongue (see page 89) as they cool, and Karin Perry's gravlax (see p. 81) as it cures.

All the above equipment is widely available from good kitchen department and kitchen shops and much of it is available by post from Lakeland Plastics Ltd (see page 136 for address).

STORE-CUPBOARD
INGREDIENTS

The following items are the basic store-cupboard ingredients which will allow you to take advantage of impulse buys or harvestings.

ANCHOVIES

Anchovy fillets in olive oil form part of many Mediterranean-type preserves in this book, so it is useful to keep a tin or two in the cupboard.

DRIED FRUIT

Always useful for making preserves, I prefer to buy those which have not been treated with mineral oil or preservatives. These types are most usually available from health food shops.

TINNED FRUIT

It's worth stocking tinned fruit both in syrup, for such things as the Quick spiced cherries on p. 27, and in unsweetened fruit juice, for making Superfast jams (see p. 66).

HERBS

Although this book gives you several recipes for preserving and blending your own herbs, I find that one or two extra items are worth having to hand, especially the blend of dried herbs known as *herbes de Provence* which contains oregano, a variety of marjoram which isn't hardy in some parts of the country. Also useful are caraway, coriander and fennel seeds, juniper berries, and dried bay leaves and chillies.

MUSTARDS

The most versatile mustards to keep in store are Dijon, coarse-grain mustard, and dry English mustard powder. It's also useful to have mustard seeds, both brown and black.

OILS

The flavour of a particular oil is an important contribution to the finished preserve or seasoning and in all the recipes which demand oil I have given a clear indication which type it should be. I would never advocate using vegetable or corn oils, which have coarse and heavy flavours, but equally the very expensive 'château-bottled' extra virgin olive oils are not necessary either, as you are adding other flavours to them. A good supermarket own-brand extra virgin olive oil has much to recommend it (I find those from Waitrose and Sainsbury's particularly satisfactory). For making spiced oils, groundnut and sunflower are suitable, and for mixing with a distinctive oil such as walnut, I like the total neutrality of grapeseed oil. All are easily available in most supermarkets and good delicatessens.

OLIVES

Tins or jars of olives in brine are invaluable store-cupboard items – they can then be transformed into something much more interesting. I like to have to hand a supply of stoned olives, as making something like Tapénade with Dried Tomatoes (see p. 47) is so much easier if you don't have to take the stones out first.

ORANGE FLOWER WATER AND ROSE-WATER

Both of these are mentioned in various recipes. They can be bought from good delicatessens and will keep for some considerable time in a dark cupboard. The soft fragrance that rose-water gives can be imitated by using highly scented rose petals, or by the leaves of rose-scented geraniums, but orange flower water is inimitable.

SALT

When it was available, I used to use Cheshire block salt for salting and brining meat. Now it is not, I have turned to sea salt, using the square crystal Maldon salt for the table, and fine or coarse sea salt in all cooking. They are all beautifully 'salty' salts, so you use less of them.

SPICES

Supermarkets are bulging now with a wonderful range of whole spices, sensibly packaged in small amounts as they do lose pungency if you keep them too long. Most of us keep such things as cloves, nutmeg and cinnamon to hand, but many of the recipes in this book mention mace (the outer husk of the nutmeg which has a distinctive, milder flavour), both whole in 'blades' and powdered; allspice (also known as Jamaica pepper and not to be confused with mixed spice), whole and powdered; peppercorns, which now come in green (both dried and in brine), and pink, as well as black and white, and as a very useful mixture of all or some of these. Ginger is now available in an excellent freeze-dried form, a good alternative to pieces of dried ginger root. Chinese five spice powder, which contains the distinctive star-anise, is also used in one or two recipes.

SUGAR

Many of the recipes, to make them quicker and easier, call for sugar-with-pectin – a great boon to the jam-maker in a hurry. It blends sugar with tartaric acid and apple pectin, and gives a good set, and beautifully clear jam or jelly, very quickly. It saves time, fuel and, most particularly, flavour. Also useful is golden granulated sugar, which gives a little of the caramelly flavour of brown sugar but is easier to use. Preserving sugar dissolves quickly, thus reducing the risk of burning.

DRIED TOMATOES

Also known as sun-dried tomatoes (and the best ones are genuinely sun-dried), these come both in their dried form and, more easily available, in oil. They have a delicious sweet flavour, the concentration of a ripe tomato, and are excellent store-cupboard items. Those in oil keep less long, as the oil will go rancid; dried will keep in the dark for up to nine months.

TINNED TOMATOES

The tomatoes I used for the Tomato jam on p. 78 are chopped tinned tomatoes, a particularly useful form.

TABASCO

This is the liquid version of cayenne pepper and much easier to use. It's invaluable for adding drop by cautious drop until you reach the desired degree of heat. A small bottle lasts for years.

VANILLA

Always go for whole vanilla pods, or vanilla extract, rather than vanilla essence. The pods are available among the spices on supermarket shelves, but sadly essence is far easier to find than extract.

VINEGARS

Few of the recipes in this book call for malt vinegar, once the staple ingredient of the traditional English pickle or chutney. This is because there are so many subtler, less harsh alternatives around and, as with the oils, I have made specific recommendations in each recipe. Supermarkets are now offering cheap versions of very expensive vinegars such as balsamic and sherry vinegar, which are perfectly acceptable when you are adding extra flavouring.

For a list of postal suppliers for some of the above ingredients see page 136.

SAVOURY PRESERVES

The pungent wafts of vinegar which used to fill houses where the late-summer chutney-making was under way is something of an old-fashioned smell now. The microwave can be used to cut down on all that long slow simmering, and, since we have other means of preservation in the form of refrigerators and deep freezes, it's no longer necessary to use gallons of fierce vinegar which had to be cooked into moderation.

Some of the recipes in this chapter are almost instant – quickly made little relishes that don't keep for more than a few weeks but add zest to any dish they accompany. Equally, many of the recipes preserve in the Mediterranean fashion, using oil to exclude air and add flavour to mixtures of olives, lemons, anchovies and so on. This may seem extravagant as I stress the use of olive oil more than any other, but you can recycle any remaining oil most successfully, using it for frying, for salad dressing, for basting and marinating – and olive oil has now proved to be one of the healthiest as well as one of the most delicious oils. If you don't like the pungent flavour (and the expense) of the extra virgin oil, there are milder options, down to the new 'light' olive oils. This type of preserve is often a dish in its own right – see the Exotic mushrooms in oil on p. 37, or Goat's cheese preserved in oil on p. 24.

For storage, use hoarded jam jars and preserving jars – well-cleaned and dried – always remembering that vinegar corrodes metal; this means lining any metal lids with waxed paper, cling film or polythene before capping any vinegary chutney or pickle. Best of all use plastic-lined lids; cellophane jam pot covers are not ideal for chutneys and pickles as they can allow the evaporation of vinegar, leaving a dry crust on top.

The higher the proportion of vinegar in the recipe, the better it will keep, as long as you take care to prevent evaporation. However, all these preserves are best eaten within a year unless otherwise stated.

Mrs beck's raw apple chutney

—— • ——

INGREDIENTS

PREPARATION TIME
15 minutes
WAITING TIME
1 week
FILLS 3 MEDIUM JARS

*25 g (1 oz) brown mustard
seeds*
225 g (8 oz) sultanas
*1 tablespoon peeled and
chopped fresh root ginger*
1 dessertspoon fine sea salt
*225 g (8 oz) demerara
sugar*
*300 ml (10 fl oz) cider
vinegar*
225 g (8 oz) onion
2 garlic cloves
*750 g (1 ½ lb) cooking
apples*

This is one of my favourite chutneys, very easy to make although you do have to exert patience while it matures. I now prefer to use fresh root ginger, which is widely available (see p. 99 for a way to preserve any you have left over), rather than dried ginger, but you can use either. This goes well with any cold meat, or any of the hard cheeses (particularly a proper Yorkshire Wensleydale). It can also accompany mildly curried dishes.

———

Put the first 6 ingredients into a large china or glass bowl and stir well until the sugar dissolves. Chop the onions and garlic very finely. Peel and core the apples and chop these coarsely, then mix onions, garlic and apples thoroughly into the vinegar mixture. Cover the bowl with cling film and leave for a week, stirring well once a day. Pot into clean dry jars and cap with plastic lids. Despite the fact that this is a raw chutney, it keeps well for up to a year, but check to see that it doesn't dry out.

FRESH APPLE AND MINT RELISH

— • —

This doesn't keep longer than a week in the fridge, but is very good and quick to make and uses ingredients that you might well have on hand in any case. I like the balance between the sour and sweet apples, but you could easily use eating apples alone – Cox's for preference, or, in summer before our home-grown fruit has appeared, the delicious Braeburn apples from New Zealand. This relish goes particularly well with smoked chicken, or made into a sandwich with a slice of ham, in buttered granary bread.

Peel and core the apples and put in the food processor together with the vinegar. Process briefly until finely chopped but not mushy – the vinegar will stop the apple from browning. Mix well with the remaining ingredients and leave for 1 hour before serving.

INGREDIENTS

PREPARATION TIME
10–15 minutes
WAITING TIME
1 hour

1 medium cooking apple
1 large eating apple
2 tablespoons cider vinegar
1 tablespoon runny honey
1 tablespoon chopped fresh mint
A pinch of salt
A pinch of ground allspice
A pinch of white pepper

BREAD AND BUTTER PICKLES

———— • ————

PREPARATION TIME
10 minutes plus overnight
COOKING TIME
5 minutes
FILLS 1 LARGE OR
2 MEDIUM JARS

*2 small cucumbers
weighing about 225 g
(8 oz) each
1 mild Spanish onion
25 g (1 oz) sea salt
150 ml (5 fl oz) white
wine vinegar
175 g (6 oz) demerara
sugar
1 tablespoon mustard seeds
1 teaspoon coriander seeds
A generous pinch of
cayenne*

This is the classic American pickle, made in vast quantities in many a household. It's easy to see why as its sweet-sour flavour is irresistible and it's good enough to make a sandwich in its own right. Be careful not to overcook the vegetables, so that they contribute a slight crispness to the pickle. There is no better accompaniment for corned beef sandwiches, hot dogs, or barbecued sausages.

————

Slice the cucumbers and onion and mix with the salt in a large bowl; tip into a colander, stand it over the bowl and leave to drain overnight. The salt will draw lots of moisture out of the vegetables. Next day, rinse the vegetables under a running cold tap and drain thoroughly (spread them out on a clean tea towel). Bring the vinegar, sugar, mustard and coriander seeds and the cayenne to the boil in a pan and add the vegetables. Then cook rapidly but briefly – for not more than 3 minutes so that the onion and cucumber remain *al dente*. Pot into warm dry jars and cap with vinegar-proof lids.

NERINE'S QUICKER PICKLED BEETROOT

——— • ———

The friend who gave me this recipe pointed out that this is quicker simply because you start with the sort of cooked beetroot you can buy at the greengrocer's and which comes ready packaged with a vinegary flavour. It does, however, taste even better if you have cooked your own, which is worth doing in quantity as cooked beetroot freezes well. This is one of the few recipes where I prefer to use malt rather than wine or cider vinegar, as it balances the sweetness well. It is delicious with thick slices of really good ham, or stirred into soured cream or yoghurt to serve with Rollmop herrings (see p. 82).

Put all the ingredients except the beetroot into a large saucepan and cook gently until the onion and apple are soft – about 15 minutes. Add the diced beetroot and simmer until the mixture is thick – about 15–20 minutes. Pot into warm dry jars with vinegar-proof lids.

INGREDIENTS

PREPARATION TIME
10 minutes
COOKING TIME
35 minutes
FILLS 3 MEDIUM JARS

350 g (12 oz) sliced cooking apple (peeled and cored weight)
1 large onion, sliced
½ teaspoon ground ginger
1 level teaspoon salt
225 g (8 oz) brown sugar
300 ml (10 fl oz) malt vinegar
750 g (1 ½ lb) diced cooked beetroot

GOAT'S CHEESE PRESERVED IN OIL

———— • ————

INGREDIENTS

PREPARATION TIME
15 minutes
WAITING TIME
2 days
FILLS 1 MEDIUM
PRESERVING JAR

About 450 g (1 lb) firm goat's cheese
About 1 teaspoon five pepper blend of peppercorns or to taste
About 2 teaspoons herbes de Provence or to taste
Mild olive oil or ⅔ grapeseed to ⅓ walnut oil

The best type of goat's cheese for this method of preservation are the small firm '*demi-sec*' type you can buy in French markets or better cheese shops over here, but any firm variety will do. A piece of this cheese makes a delicious snack with some crusty bread and a few olives and tomatoes; or a sophisticated last-minute starter, on a bed of mixed salad leaves. You do need good oil, such as a mild olive oil, or a mixture of grapeseed and walnut oil. Try serving these as a 'Greek Rarebit' – lightly toast some slices of olive oil bread, rub each with a cut clove of garlic, then top each with a piece of this preserved cheese and grill until bubbling. Serve hot with a glass of a robust and earthy red wine.

If necessary, cut the cheese into neat pieces about 2.5 cm (1 inch) square and spread them out in a single layer on a plate. Crush the peppercorns finely and, together with the *herbes de Provence*, sprinkle lightly over the cheeses or cheese pieces. Half fill a preserving jar with your chosen oil or oils and then add the cheese. Top up with more oil if necessary. Cap firmly and keep in the fridge for at least 2 days before eating. Bring to room temperature before serving. They will keep for about 6 weeks.

PEN-FRIEND'S
PICKLED CABBAGE

— • —

The friend who gave me this recipe was given it by her daughter's German pen-friend, who pointed out that it was really the raw version of the red-cabbage-with-apple dish that is the classic accompaniment to their Christmas goose. It certainly makes a delicious variation on our own more usual pickled red cabbage, but in the same way it is better to eat this within about three months, or the cabbage goes soggy. This goes perfectly with cold goose, of course, or any rich cold meat such as pork, especially the Salt pork on p. 90.

Shred the cabbage and the onion finely and toss them in a colander with the salt. Stand this over a plate or bowl and leave to drain overnight. Next day, rinse the cabbage and onion, tip out onto a clean towel and pat dry. Bring the vinegar to the boil with the sugar and spices, then draw aside to infuse while you core the apples and chop them coarsely (no need to peel them). Layer the cabbage and onion mixture with the apples in clean and dry preserving jars, then pour over the strained, cooled vinegar. Cap firmly, then leave at least a week before eating.

INGREDIENTS

PREPARATION TIME
10 minutes plus overnight
COOKING TIME
2–3 minutes
WAITING TIME
1 week
FILLS 2 MEDIUM
PRESERVING JARS

1 red cabbage weighing about 750 g (1 ½ lb)
1 large mild onion
25 g (1 oz) sea salt
600 ml (1 pint) white wine or cider vinegar
50 g (2 oz) brown sugar
1 tablespoon coriander seeds
2 cloves
4 eating apples

CHINOISERIE CHUTNEY

———— • ————

PREPARATION TIME
20 minutes
COOKING TIME
23 minutes
FILLS 3 SMALL JARS

6 slightly unripe kiwi fruit
1 large mild Spanish onion
2 cloves garlic
Juice and grated rind of
* 1 lime*
1 heaped teaspoon peeled
* and chopped fresh root*
* ginger*
1 green chilli, de-seeded
* and finely sliced*
65 ml (2 ½ fl oz) white
* wine vinegar*
25 g (1 oz) creamed
* coconut*
100 g (4 oz) brown sugar
1 heaped teaspoon Chinese
* five spice powder*
A few drops green food
* colouring (optional)*

Kiwi fruit have become far cheaper since they fell out of fashion. They give this chutney a sharp fresh flavour which I have balanced with the mildness of a little coconut. The Chinese flavouring, and the name, is a nod to the country where the kiwi, *Actinidia chinensis*, or Chinese gooseberry, originated. Unfortunately the bright green colouring disappears but if you miss that you can add a drop or two of food colouring. This can be made without a microwave by simmering the fruit in an open pan until soft, which will take about 15 minutes, then adding the remaining ingredients and simmering until thick and syrupy for a further 35 minutes. This tart and refreshing chutney goes well with fish and chicken dishes, especially those cooked in the Chinese style.

▬▬▬▬▬▬

Peel and chop the kiwi fruit coarsely, discarding the tough bit around the stalk area. Chop the onion and garlic finely (best done in the food processor). Put all into a large microwaveable bowl together with the juice and rind of the lime, the ginger and chilli. Cook, covered, on HIGH for 8 minutes or until soft, stirring once. Meanwhile, warm the vinegar a little and dissolve the creamed coconut in it.

Take the bowl from the microwave, drain off almost all the liquid and replace it with the vinegar and coconut mixture then add the sugar and five spice powder. Return the bowl to the microwave without covering it this time and cook on HIGH for 15 minutes, or until the chutney is thickened and syrupy, stirring once or twice. Add the food colouring, if using, at this point. Pot at once in warmed jars.

QUICK SPICED CHERRIES

——— • ———

This makes a very useful and delicious last-minute addition to the Christmas buffet and is simplicity itself. It keeps well, although it's best to refrigerate it after opening. In this case you need the cherries canned in syrup, rather than in fruit juice. It's good with any cold meat, especially tongue, ham and venison. Add a spoonful of the syrup to flavour gravies for game or to add a bit of zest to a bland casserole.

———

Put the spices into a spice ball or tie them in a piece of muslin and then in a pan with the vinegar, the syrup drained from the cherries, and the raisins. Bring to a simmer and continue to simmer fast for about 10 minutes until the mixture tastes sufficiently spicy and the vinegar has evaporated a little; add a little muscovado or moist brown sugar if you feel it isn't sweet enough. Remove the spices, add the drained cherries and heat for a further 5 minutes, then pour into warmed jars and cap tightly with vinegar-proof lids.

INGREDIENTS

PREPARATION TIME
5 minutes
COOKING TIME
15 minutes
FILLS 2 SMALL JARS

6 black peppercorns
Piece of whole nutmeg
Small piece of dried ginger
Short length of cinnamon stick
150 ml (5 fl oz) red wine vinegar
1 × 411 g (14½ oz) can pitted black cherries in syrup
75 g (3 oz) raisins

COURGETTE CHUTNEY

INGREDIENTS

PREPARATION TIME
10 minutes plus overnight
COOKING TIME
45 minutes
FILLS 3 MEDIUM JARS

*750 g (1 ½ lb) courgettes,
thickly sliced*
2 tablespoons salt
225 g (8 oz) chopped onion
3 garlic cloves, chopped
*350 g (12 oz) muscovado
sugar*
*900 ml (1 ½ pints) red wine
vinegar*
225 g (8 oz) raisins
*1 tablespoon coriander
seeds*
*2 tablespoons brown
mustard seeds*
*1 tablespoon peeled and
chopped fresh root ginger*
2 dried chillies

A good recipe to use up a glut of garden courgettes, or to make when shop courgettes are cheap. You can use green tomatoes in place of the courgettes in this recipe, or a mixture of the two if you prefer. Serve this chutney with cold lamb, or with a lamb curry. It also makes a good glaze for roast shoulder of lamb, or a corn-fed chicken. Just spoon it over the roast about 20 minutes before the end of the cooking time.

Sprinkle the courgette slices with half of the salt and leave to drain in a colander overnight. Next day, rinse, drain and pat dry. Put into a large heavy pan with the onion, garlic, remaining salt, sugar and vinegar and cook gently for about 15 minutes, until the sugar has dissolved and the vegetables have softened. Add the raisins, spices, ginger and chillies, stir well and cook at a steady simmer for another 25 minutes or until the mixture is thick, stirring frequently. Take it out and stir half-way through the cooking time. Pot into warm dry jars.

FRESH CORN RELISH

— • —

When cobs are cheap, or if you've grown your own, this relish really comes into its own since it's so much nicer made with the fresh, sweet, juicy kernels. Detaching the kernels from the cobs is easy and quick – simply stand the cob on end in a bowl, hold it with one hand and run a sharp knife down against the stalk with the other so that the kernels are sliced off into the bowl. (If you use a flat plate or board, you are likely to end up with kernels in unexpected corners of the kitchen.) If you must have an even quicker version, use a 450 g (1 lb) bag of frozen corn, but it won't be as good. Lovely with barbecued chicken and sausages, or take on picnics as a dip for cold sausages and chicken legs – it's very popular with children.

Detach the kernels from the cobs, skin and roughly chop the tomatoes, chop the pepper finely, discarding the seeds or not as you like (depending on whether you want to add their peppery flavour), and slice the onion into fine rings. Put all the vegetables into a thick-bottomed pan and cook, covered, over a low heat, without any further liquid until all are soft – about 15 minutes. Don't add the salt at this stage as it hardens the corn kernels; there should be enough liquid from the tomatoes and onion to prevent burning, but give the contents of the pan a stir from time to time to make sure. Then stir in the sugar, salt, mustard, cider vinegar and the water and cook at a simmer, uncovered, for a further 15 minutes, until the mixture has thickened a little. Pot in warm, dry jars.

INGREDIENTS

PREPARATION TIME
25 minutes
COOKING TIME
30 minutes
FILLS 3 MEDIUM JARS

4 large fresh corn cobs
2 large well-flavoured
  tomatoes
1 large red pepper
1 medium onion
50 g (2 oz) golden
  granulated sugar
2 teaspoons salt
1 dessertspoon mustard
  powder
150 ml (5 fl oz) cider
  vinegar
Scant 150 ml (5 fl oz)
  water

SPICY DAMSON RELISH

—— • ——

INGREDIENTS

PREPARATION TIME
*2 minutes with a food mill
or 10 minutes without*
COOKING TIME
30 minutes

450 g (1 lb) damsons
150 ml (5 fl oz) dry sherry
1 garlic clove
1 teaspoon salt
225 g (8 oz) muscovado
  sugar
1 teaspoon peeled and
  finely chopped fresh root
  ginger
5 drops Tabasco

There is no better plum for jam, jellies and relishes than the damson, because of its concentrated, almost spicy, flavour. This recipe is inspired by a sauce given by the late Jeremy Round in his book *The Independent Cook*. It doesn't keep for all that long so I don't make it in large quantities. However, it is quick to make and frozen damsons work just as well as fresh ones – just cook them from frozen, allowing a little longer for the initial cooking. This relish can accompany grilled duck breasts, roast duck (stir into the gravy). Add a spoonful or two to venison casserole, or add ½ teaspoon to a vinaigrette for a salad of mixed bitter leaves.

Cook the damsons with the sherry until soft, which will take about 10 minutes. Push through a food mill or through a sieve, extracting the stones as you go. Work the garlic clove to a paste with the salt, using the point of a knife on a board. Return the damsons to the pan with all the other ingredients including the garlic. Simmer gently, for about 20 minutes, until thick. Pour into a warm dry jar and add a teaspoon or so of sherry to cover the surface.

CUMBRIAN SAUCE

——— • ———

Cumberland sauce, that well-known mixture of redcurrant jelly and port, did not originate in the county of Cumberland. There is a plausible story that it was named after the Duke of Cumberland, brother of George IV, who became ruler of Hanover; certainly fruit sauces with meat, particularly with game, were then popular in Germany. I learnt to make it when living in Cumberland, and to serve it with thick slices of superlative Cumberland ham, but I often made my own version using rowan jelly – as rowans grow everywhere on the Cumbrian fells – instead of redcurrant and I still prefer to do this, so I rechristened it. The recipe for Rowan jelly is on p. 48, but you can compromise with a good quality bought redcurrant jelly.

This sauce goes well not just with ham, but with pork and game pies, cold duck, pâtés and terrines, and it does wonders for all that post-Christmas cold turkey.

———

Scrub the fruit, and remove the peel as thinly as possible. Cut the peel into thin matchsticks, put it in a pan, cover with cold water, bring to the boil and boil for 2 minutes. Drain, cover with more cold water, boil again and keep boiling for 3 minutes. Drain well and put the peel to one side. This process removes the bitterness of the peel, as well as making it soft enough to make pleasant eating.

Put the rowan or redcurrant jelly in the warm pan and put it to melt over a low heat, stirring in the remaining ingredients and then the blanched orange and lemon peel. When all the jelly has melted and blended with the port, decant into warm dry jars. It will keep for several weeks in the fridge.

INGREDIENTS

PREPARATION TIME
20 minutes
COOKING TIME
10 minutes
FILLS 2 SMALL JARS

2 oranges
1 lemon
225 g (8 oz) rowan or
    redcurrant jelly
150 ml (5 fl oz) port
1 teaspoon coarse-grained
    mustard
A pinch of ground ginger

PICKLED EGGS

— • —

INGREDIENTS

PREPARATION TIME
5 minutes
COOKING TIME
10 minutes
WAITING TIME
1 week
FILLS 2 LARGE
PRESERVING JARS

12 hard-boiled eggs, shelled
15 g (½ oz) mixed
  peppercorns
2 dried chillies
1 dessertspoon peeled and
  chopped fresh root ginger
  (optional)
2 garlic cloves, crushed
  (optional)
1 dessertspoon salt
900 ml (1 ½ pints) cider or
  white wine vinegar

No larder is complete without a jar of these – they are invaluable for instant packed lunches or picnics and can even make a quick snack partnered with buttered crispbread. I have brought the seasonings for the spiced vinegar up to date, but you can omit the garlic and use dried ginger if you prefer a more traditional flavour. They keep safely for at least 6 months. It's best not to use new-laid eggs for this recipe as they are very difficult to peel neatly. For a really modish present, try using quail eggs – but allow plenty of peeling time as they are fiddly to do. Pickled eggs accompany vegetable curries and spiced rice dishes very well – and contribute to the protein content at the same time.

Put the eggs into clean dry jars. Then put all the spices, the ginger, garlic and salt, together with the vinegar, into a large pan, bring to the boil, then lower the heat and simmer gently for about 10 minutes, or until the vinegar is spiced to your liking. Remove from the heat and allow to get quite cold before straining and pouring over the eggs, which should be totally immersed. If you find they are not, add enough cold vinegar to achieve this.

NERINE'S QUICKER PICKLED BEETROOT (*page 23*)

FRESH CORN RELISH (*page 29*)

Fierce garlic paste

—— • ——

This fiery concoction is not for the timid, but delights garlic *aficionados*. It is an ideal condiment for adding zest to all sorts of dishes and is best made with new season's garlic in about August or September when it is juicy and sweet. Fork it into a plain pilaff, add a little to crème fraîche, fromage frais, yoghurt or mayonnaise to provide an instant dip for crudités or spread thinly over fish steaks before baking or grilling.

———

Put all the ingredients into a food processor or blender and process until as fine as possible, stopping the machine to push the ingredients down onto the blades if necessary. Pack into a clean, dry jar and pour a little more oil over the top. This will keep, under its oil seal, for about 2 months.

INGREDIENTS

PREPARATION TIME
10 minutes
FILLS 1 VERY SMALL JAR

*1 head garlic, each clove
  separated and peeled*
2 teaspoons ground cumin
*2 teaspoons ground
  coriander*
*2 teaspoons ground black
  pepper*
*1 tablespoon peeled and
  chopped fresh root ginger*
*1 fresh green chilli,
  de-seeded*
4 tablespoons sunflower oil
Juice of ½ lime
A pinch of sugar

PRESERVED LEMONS AND OLIVES (*page 36*)

PLUM AND ROSEMARY JELLY (*page 42*)

PRESERVED
LEMONS AND OLIVES

— • —

INGREDIENTS

PREPARATION TIME
10 minutes
WAITING TIME
1 month
FILLS 2–3 MEDIUM JARS

*3 thin-skinned unwaxed
or organically grown
lemons*
*1 × 400g (14oz) can
pitted black olives in
brine*
*150–250 ml (5–8 fl oz)
extra virgin olive oil*
4 teaspoons coarse sea salt
*3 cloves finely chopped
garlic*
*1 teaspoon dried herbes de
Provence mixture*

Lemons preserved in salt are a traditional Middle Eastern store-cupboard item. I have combined this with the Mediterranean method of preserving olives to produce something which is ethnically hybrid, but has a very useful role as an hors d'oeuvre ingredient. If you can get unwaxed, or organically grown, lemons I would suggest you use those instead of the waxed and sprayed kind – you are eating a lot of the peel in this recipe.

To accompany this very Mediterranean-flavoured preserve, serve some slices of goat's cheese, or curls of Parmesan, a good robust salami, or air-dried ham such as Parma or Serrano, or simply hard-boiled eggs. It's also very good with freshly grilled sardines. Use the remaining olive oil as a baste for grilled fish or chicken.

Wash the lemons (whatever their type) and dry well, then slice fairly thinly, removing pips as you meet them. Drain the olives and cut each one in half. Pour a little olive oil over the bottom of a clean, dry preserving jar, sprinkle generously with salt, less generously with some of the chopped garlic and *herbes de Provence* and put in your first layer of lemon slices. Cover with a layer of olives, add another sprinkling of salt, garlic and *herbes* and continue like this until the jar is full. Finish with a lemon layer and pour in oil to cover. (You can be very relaxed about quantities in this recipe.) Leave a month before eating, by which time the lemon will have lost its bitterness and have an intriguing mellowness.

Exotic
MUSHROOMS IN OIL

—— • ——

This is a preserve I make every so often when I find that the supermarket pack of exotic mushrooms I've bought contains too many for the recipe I'm doing. Rather than freeze them, I treat them as follows, to bring out as part of an emergency starter. I give the method without the quantities, since these are immaterial. These are good all on their own with some warmed brown rolls, and have a great affinity with cold roast beef.

Wipe the mushrooms and trim off any tough pieces at the end of the stalks. Cut into neatish pieces, then place in a steamer, sprinkle lightly with salt and steam over boiling water until just tender – usually about 5–7 minutes depending on the variety. At the same time add some peeled and halved garlic cloves to cook in the water below the mushrooms. Drain both mushrooms and garlic on kitchen paper, then pack into clean, dry jars. Add a teaspoon of lightly crushed coriander seeds, a sprig of thyme and a bay leaf to each jar and top up with olive oil. To serve, pour off some of the oil into a separate container (and use for frying potatoes, or strips of bacon to add to a salad), tip the mushrooms into a dish, add a squeeze of lemon juice and a grinding of pepper.

INGREDIENTS

PREPARATION TIME
5 minutes
COOKING TIME
5–7 minutes
WAITING TIME
24 hours

Exotic mushrooms, such as oyster, shiitake, ceps, chestnut (also called brown cap)
Salt
Garlic
Coriander seeds
Sprigs of fresh thyme
Bay leaves
Olive oil

Olives cassées

— • —

INGREDIENTS

PREPARATION TIME
15 minutes
WAITING TIME
1 week
FILLS 2 MEDIUM JARS

*225 g (8 oz) large green
olives*
*4 large garlic cloves, finely
chopped*
*A generous tablespoon
fennel seeds*
1 teaspoon coarse sea salt
*About 300 ml (10 fl oz)
extra virgin olive oil*

When we are staying with friends in Provence, we make a point of visiting the Saturday market in Aix, of buying a generous scoop of these *olives cassées*, and of sitting in the sun on the steps of the town hall to eat them. A word of warning – the crushed olives look deceptively soft, but as it's possible to break a tooth on the hidden stones, it's best to warn the unwary that they are there. These olives are delicious on their own with a glass of robust red Lubéron wine, or as part of a mixed hors d'oeuvre. Again, you can keep the remaining oil to use in salad dressings.

Rinse the olives of their brine, then tip them on to a plate lined with paper towels to drain. Crush each olive with a steak mallet or, best of all, an ordinary hammer – I wrap the head thoroughly in cling film and then tie a clean handkerchief round it and find that works well, especially if you put the olives on a wooden board so that they don't slip. The flesh of the olive should crack, but the stone should remain intact. Then just pile the olives into a dry, clean jar, add the seasonings, top with the olive oil and cap tightly. Shake the jar well, and do that daily for the week you will have to wait before you can eat them.

ORANGE AND THYME JELLY

—— • ——

A clear golden jelly fragrant with thyme which makes an ideal present as it can be used for so many things. I like to make it with a light set so that it will melt quickly into a sauce or salad dressing. Try to use fresh thyme if you can, but if you have to use dried halve the quantities. This jelly is delicious with cold salmon, either on its own or added to mayonnaise, and with chicken liver pâté. Or use it to glaze chicken joints before baking in the oven.

———

Add the lemon juice to the orange juice in a measuring jug, and add more orange juice, if necessary, to bring the total quantity of juice up to 600 ml (1 pint). Put the juices into a pan with the thyme, bring slowly to the boil, then put a lid on the pan, draw off the heat and leave to infuse overnight, or until cold and the liquid is well-flavoured with thyme. Take out the sprigs, remove some of the leaves and put the leaves in a large pan with the juice and sugar. Bring slowly to the boil and then boil hard for 1 minute before testing for setting (see p. 10), boiling for another minute if you prefer a firmer set. Pot into warm, dry jars.

INGREDIENTS

PREPARATION TIME
5–6 minutes
COOKING TIME
Overnight plus 1 minute
FILLS 4 SMALL JARS

Juice of 1 large juicy lemon
About 450 ml (15 fl oz)
*   unsweetened orange juice*
5 sprigs thyme, about
*   10 cm (4 inches) long*
About 450 g (1 lb)
*   sugar-with-pectin*

SWEET AND SOUR ONIONS

———— • ————

INGREDIENTS

PREPARATION TIME
5 minutes (or 20 if using onions in their skins)
COOKING TIME
20 minutes
FILLS 1 LARGE
PRESERVING JAR

450 g (1 lb) ready-prepared frozen button onions
About 4 tablespoons olive oil
Pinch brown sugar
Salt and freshly ground pepper
3 tablespoons balsamic vinegar
2 bay leaves

Some delicatessens sell these typically Italian onions as part of their range of *antipasti*, but they are easy to make at home and will keep well for up to a month. They are very different from our more aggressive pickled onions, especially in this recipe where I use balsamic vinegar to give them a particularly mellow sweetness. To save time I have suggested using ready-prepared button onions which can be found in the freezer cabinet of large supermarkets and freezer centres, but if you can't get these, part-cook the button or pickling onions in their skins first so that the whole operation is easier and quicker and far less tear-jerking.

Simmer the onions, without defrosting them, for 10 minutes in salted water, then drain and pat dry on paper towels. If using fresh onions, cook for a further 5 minutes then drain and peel when cool enough to handle. In a heavy frying pan, which will hold the onions in a single layer, heat 2 tablespoons of the oil over a low heat, add the onions, sugar, a very little salt and a generous grinding of pepper and cook gently for 5 minutes, turning the onions once or twice. Add the vinegar and the bay leaves, raise the heat a little and cook briefly, stirring all the time, until the vinegar and pan juices have amalgamated into a syrup and the onions are well coated. Remove from the heat and allow to cool. Spoon into the jar and add the remaining oil to cover – you may need more than indicated, depending on the size of the jar, and of the onions. You can eat these at once without the final addition of oil. If you do store them for longer, keep in a cool place or in the least cold part of the fridge, removing them to room temperature for 15 minutes before serving.

RED PEPPER AND TOMATO PRESERVE

— • —

This preserve makes use of the fruit and vegetables of early autumn, but makes a change from usual late-summer chutneys as it is more like a savoury jam, with a set consistency. Using the apples provides the necessary pectin and sharpens the flavour a little. You may find that you have some of the tomato and apple juice left over, depending on the ripeness of the fruit and how juicy it proved to be. If so, use it to make some herb-flavoured jellies (follow the method on p. 39 for Orange and thyme jelly). This preserve is delicious in roast beef sandwiches or add a spoonful to tomato sauces for pasta dishes. Also a good relish to serve with barbecued sausages or hamburgers.

Remove any bruised bits from the apples, then cut them into chunks without bothering to peel or core; chop the tomatoes roughly, again without bothering to peel, and put both apples and tomatoes into a pan with just enough water to cover, then cook gently until soft. Tip into a jelly bag and leave to drip overnight. Next day, take 900 ml (1½ pints) of this apple and tomato juice and put it into a large pan, together with the washed and finely chopped peppers (don't discard all the seeds, but leave some in to give a peppery flavour to the preserve), the garlic, and the bay leaves. Cook, covered, over a gentle heat until the peppers are soft (about 20 minutes). Stir in the sugar and bring to a rolling boil, then boil hard, testing for setting point after 3 minutes (see p. 10). Stir in the vinegar to taste, then leave to stand a little before stirring to distribute the peppers throughout the preserve, and potting into warm, dry jars. Remove the bay leaves if you wish.

INGREDIENTS

PREPARATION TIME
20 minutes plus overnight
COOKING TIME
30 minutes
FILLS 3 MEDIUM JARS

900 g (2 lb) windfall apples, or *450 g (1 lb) eating apples and 450 g (1 lb) cooking apples*
750 g (1½ lb) ripe, well-flavoured tomatoes
750 g (1½ lb) red peppers
6 garlic cloves, finely chopped
3 fresh bay leaves, or *1½ dried*
450 g (1 lb) golden granulated sugar
2–3 tablespoons sherry or *balsamic vinegar*

Plum and Rosemary Jelly

— • —

INGREDIENTS

PREPARATION TIME
5 minutes
COOKING TIME
35–40 minutes
FILLS APPROX. 4
MEDIUM JARS

1.5 kg (3 lb) plums
1 bag preserving sugar
  (see method)
3 generous sprigs of
  rosemary

Our nextdoor neighbour has a prolific Victoria plum tree and is generous with the fruit. We have several flourishing rosemary bushes. Put the two together and you have a lovely rich and fragrant jelly for savoury uses. The plums shouldn't be too ripe and you can use a mixture of ripe and unripe fruit. This jelly accompanies cold pork well, and is delicious with chicken liver pâté, or a pork terrine; you can also use it as a plum sauce in Chinese recipes.

Put the plums in a pan with enough water to come just below the top layer of fruit. Cover and cook gently until the fruit is soft – about 10–15 minutes. Tip into a jelly bag and leave to drip overnight. Next day, measure the juice and put it into a preserving pan with 450 g (1 lb) sugar to 600 ml (1 pint) juice. Strip the rosemary leaves from their stalks, then chop them small and add to the sugar and juice in the pan. Bring slowly to the boil, then boil fast to setting point (see p. 10) – about 8 minutes. Draw aside and leave for about 15 minutes, then stir well to distribute the rosemary throughout the jelly, and pour into warm, dry jars.

MRS BEETON'S 'EXCELLENT PICKLE'

——— • ———

It's interesting to note that this has been omitted from the latest edition of Mrs Beeton, as its combination of flavours are very appealing to our modern palates. I haven't tried to 'keep it a year', as she notes, as our batch was eaten pretty quickly, but judging by the amount of alcohol and vinegar, it is quite likely that it might. The wineglass I used for measuring held 150 ml (5 fl oz). This pickle is good with oriental-style chicken dishes, barbecued lamb chops, and stir-fries.

Layer the cucumber, apples and onion in a clean, dry jar, sprinkling each layer with a little cayenne as you go. Mix the sherry with the soy sauce and pour this into the jar, then top up with the cider vinegar. 'It will be fit for use the day it is made.'

INGREDIENTS

PREPARATION TIME
15 minutes
FILLS 1 LARGE
PRESERVING JAR

1 large cucumber, thinly sliced
2 small Bramley apples, peeled, cored and thinly sliced
1 mild Spanish onion, thinly sliced
¾ teaspoon cayenne
1 wineglassful light soy sauce
1 wineglassful medium dry sherry
About 150 ml (5 fl oz) cider vinegar

PINEAPPLE RELISH

—— • ——

INGREDIENTS

PREPARATION TIME
15 minutes
WAITING TIME
1 hour

1 *miniature pineapple*
1 *garlic clove*
A *pinch of salt*
½ *teaspoon chilli powder*
½ *teaspoon black mustard
seeds*
1 *teaspoon peeled and
chopped fresh root ginger*
2 *teaspoons white wine
vinegar*

A very simple and quick recipe which will not keep long – although I found it lasted a fortnight when stored in the fridge. If you can't find one of the mini-pineapples that I used for this recipe, use half a medium one, cut the remainder into neat pieces, sugar lightly and freeze for a subsequent fruit salad or to go with ice-cream. Use the relish to accompany curries or spicy barbecue dishes. It is especially good with chicken fried in a spiced breadcrumb coating.

Peel and dice the pineapple as finely as possible. Work the garlic to a paste with the salt, using a knife blade on a plate, then mix this and all the other ingredients with the pineapple. Allow to stand for at least an hour before serving.

SPICED PEARS

⸺ • ⸺

This was my mother's recipe for using at least some of the hundreds of small hard pears yielded every year without fail by an old pear tree in the garden. For this recipe you can use hard characterless pears – the unripe Conference variety as sold by most supermarkets does perfectly – they gain character by this treatment. These pears accompany cold pork or tongue particularly well; try using a little of the vinegar as the basis of a dressing for coleslaw, or potato salads.

─────

Peel the pears but keep them whole and leave the stalks on, and stick each with a clove. While you are peeling the fruit, bring the vinegar, sugar, lightly crushed spices and cinnamon stick to the boil in a wide pan and then simmer for 5 minutes. Add the pears, cover the pan and simmer gently for about 25 minutes or until the fruit is transparent and tender. Take out the pears and put into the warmed, dry jars. Then pour the hot spiced vinegar over them. I prefer to leave the spices in, but you can strain them out.

INGREDIENTS

PREPARATION TIME
15 minutes
COOKING TIME
30 minutes
WAITING TIME
1 month
FILLS 2 LARGE
PRESERVING JARS

─────

750 g (1 ½ lb) hard pears
750 ml (1 ¼ pints) cider vinegar
150 g (5 oz) brown sugar
4 cardamom pods, lightly crushed
2 teaspoons coriander seeds, lightly crushed
5 cm (2 inch) piece of cinnamon stick
Cloves

APULIAN
TOMATO PRESERVE

— • —

INGREDIENTS

PREPARATION TIME
10 minutes
WAITING TIME
1 week
FILLS 1–2 SMALL JARS

25 g (1 oz) anchovy fillets
4 garlic cloves, peeled
15 g (½ oz) capers
1 teaspoon fennel seeds,
lightly crushed
25 g (1 oz) dried tomatoes,
snipped into strips
About 120 ml (4 fl oz)
olive oil

The idea for this recipe came when I was reading Constance Gray's *Honey from a Weed*, in which she gives an evocative description of drying tomatoes under the hot Apulian sun, before layering them with salted anchovies. My recipe is not as evocative, involving a trip to the Italian deli if you have one, or your supermarket if you haven't, but it still tastes so good that I have to stop myself from raiding the jar whenever I'm hungry. I have used ordinary dried tomatoes here, but you can use those which have already been preserved in oil, in which case the preserve will be ready to eat in hours, rather than days. Use it to accompany crudités, toasted olive oil bread or grilled goat's cheese. It is an invaluable hors d'oeuvre ingredient and tastes extra good spooned into baked potatoes.

Chop the anchovies, garlic and capers roughly, then mix with the fennel seeds. Spread a teaspoonful of this mixture over the base of the clean, dry jar, cover with a layer of dried tomato strips, top these with a layer of the anchovy mixture and continue until all the ingredients are used up – no salt is necessary because of the anchovies. Pour over enough olive oil to cover the top layer, cap and leave in a cool place for at least a week.

TAPÉNADE WITH DRIED TOMATOES

—— • ——

Tapénade, a paste made predominantly of black olives, and sometimes with anchovies and capers as well, is often served with quarters of hard-boiled egg as part of a Provençal starter. Once dried tomatoes in oil became widely available in the better supermarkets, I tried adding a few to the traditional Provençal recipe and found that they contributed a rich sweetness that seems entirely appropriate. Although the amounts of orange flower water and cognac are tiny, they can nevertheless be detected amongst the stronger flavours and contribute to the dish. Tapénade, with or without the dried tomatoes, is an invaluable standby which will keep, once made up and topped with oil to exclude the air, for at least a month in the fridge. It's not cheap to make, but a little goes a long way as the flavour is so concentrated. Spread it on toasted olive oil bread rubbed with a clove of garlic, for a quick snack. Or insert teaspoonfuls of this under the skin of a chicken before roasting it in the usual way.

———

Put all the ingredients except the last three into the blender or food processor, and blend or process to as smooth a paste as you can. Add the orange flower water and the cognac or brandy and blend briefly, then, with the motor still running, add the olive oil in a thin stream. Spoon into a dish if you are serving it at once, or into a clean, dry jar, with a little olive oil poured over the surface if you want to store it.

INGREDIENTS

PREPARATION TIME
15 minutes
FILLS 1 MEDIUM JAR

200 g (7 oz) pitted black olives
50 g (2 oz) dried tomatoes in oil
1 tin anchovy fillets in oil
25 g (1 oz) capers, drained
1 teaspoon coarse-grain mustard
2 garlic cloves, peeled
A generous grinding of black pepper
A pinch of ground allspice
1 teaspoon orange flower water
1 teaspoon cognac or brandy
About 75 ml (2 ½ fl oz) extra virgin olive oil

ROWAN JELLY

——— • ———

INGREDIENTS

PREPARATION TIME
Overnight
COOKING TIME
40 minutes
WAITING TIME
3 months
EACH 600 ML
(1 PINT) JUICE
WILL FILL 2 MEDIUM
JARS

*About 2 kg (4 ½ lb) or a
basketful of ripe rowan
berries*
*About 2 litres (3 ½ pints)
water*
About 1.5 kg (3 lb) sugar

To my mind quite the best jelly to serve with any meat. Rowans grow prolifically anywhere where there is acid soil, seemingly just as happy on Surrey heaths as on Cumbrian fells and just as content in suburban gardens as in wilder habitats. So although you'll never find them for sale, finding them growing wild is quite easy. Pick them when they are bright red, in late summer and early autumn, and don't stint yourself as rowan jelly definitely improves with age. Most recipes include some apple as there is very little pectin in rowan berries, but I prefer the unadulterated smokey, tart flavour of the rowans themselves and therefore tolerate the soft set that results.

Rowan jelly accompanies anything that you might use redcurrant jelly for, but with greater subtlety. It is excellent with lamb and even better with mutton, delicious with hare and venison and pigeon.

Don't bother to remove the berries from the stalks – just take out any leaves, rinse the fruit and put into a large pan with just enough water to show below the top layer of berries. Bring to a gentle boil, lower the heat and simmer for about 20 minutes or until the berries are soft. Tip into a jelly bag and leave to drip overnight into a large bowl. Next day, measure the liquid into a preserving pan and add 450 g (1 lb) sugar to each 600 ml (1 pint) juice. Bring slowly to the boil, then boil hard until setting point (see p. 10) is reached – about 20 minutes but test after 10, as much will depend on how wet or dry the growing season has been. Pot into warm, dry jars and leave for at least 3 months before eating. Hide a few at the back of the cupboard so that you can experience the quality of a five-year-old jar of this superlative jelly.

S W E E T P R E S E R V E S

Jam-making can be a terrible chore, and if you make jam simply to use up a glut of a not-very-interesting fruit, then it can produce a glut of not-very-interesting jam, jars of which will haunt your larder shelves for years to come. But in this chapter I give recipes for making small quantities of jams, jellies and sweet preserves, very easily and in some cases taking only a few minutes.

What has revolutionized jam-making is the advent of sugar-with-pectin, which means that, on average, a jelly will reach setting point in 1 minute, a jam in 4 minutes, timed from the point at which the jam comes to a full boil (for a definition of this see p. 10). This sugar is expensive, but you waste less fruit and juice in evaporation and the fuel costs are also lower. The flavour is fresher and clearer, too. As jam made this fast won't keep as long, it is even more important to make sure that jam jars are scrupulously clean and dry and warmed before filling, and for many of the jams I advise keeping them in the fridge once you have started a jar.

And jam isn't just for tea; I have given alternative uses in each recipe. Many of them, especially the fruits preserved in syrup, make excellent presents, so it is a good idea to hoard any extra-decorative jars, or to buy wide-mouthed glass preserving jars with hinged lids – the half-litre size is particularly useful.

DRIED APRICOT AND LEMON JAM

——— • ———

PREPARATION TIME
5 minutes plus overnight
COOKING TIME
35–40 minutes
FILLS 3–4 MEDIUM JARS

750 g (1 ½ lb) dried apricots
900 ml (1 ½ pints) water
Juice and grated rind of 2
  large lemons
1 vanilla pod or 1
  teaspoon vanilla extract
750 g (1 ½ lb) sugar-with-
  pectin

The pronounced flavour of dried apricots is here underlined with lemon and vanilla, producing a rich-tasting preserve made with the minimum of effort. If you can get untreated dried fruit from a health-food shop, the flavour will be even better. If you use a vanilla pod, wash it after use, dry out in a low oven and replace in its jar. You could use vanilla extract instead but not vanilla essence.

This is the classic apricot jam, ideal for melting down before brushing over a fruit cake that is to have a marzipan covering, or use it to glaze fruit flans. Brush it over the base of a flan case before filling with fruit and cream, or use it to sandwich rich chocolate cakes.

Put the apricots in a large bowl and cover with the water. Leave in a cool place overnight. Next day, tip into a preserving pan and add the lemon juice and rind and the vanilla. Simmer gently until the apricots are soft – about 15–20 minutes, depending on the quality of the fruit. Add the sugar and bring to a full boil, then boil hard for 4 minutes, stirring often. Test for setting (see p. 10). Draw aside for 15 minutes before potting into warm, dry jars.

SPICED
APPLE HONEY

—— • ——

This is a really quick and easy and very cheap preserve to make in the windfall season. I use a cheap 'every-day' clear honey for this, the kind that comes in bumper jars from the supermarket. If you can't get dried root ginger, use freeze-dried ginger instead; powdered spices tend to make the jelly cloudy. It's a very useful preserve – good on cinnamon toast for tea, fine for a cold (a table-spoon in a mug of hot water, plus a shot of whisky), or use a tiny amount to enliven the dressing for coleslaw or an apple and celery salad.

■■■

Wash the apples and remove any bad or bruised bits, then chop roughly without peeling or coring. Put into a pre-serving pan with 600 ml (1 pint) water to each 900 g (2 lb) fruit and simmer gently until the apples are soft and floppy. Tip into a jelly bag and leave to drip overnight. Next day, measure the juice into a preserving pan and to each 600 ml (1 pint), add 350 g (12 oz) sugar, 100 g (4 oz) honey, and 3 cloves, a small piece of ginger root and about 5 cm (2 inch) cinnamon stick, tied in a piece of muslin or put into a spice ball. Bring slowly to the boil (to melt the sugar), then boil fast to set (see p. 10) – test after 4 minutes. Remover the spices and pot in warm, dry jars.

INGREDIENTS

PREPARATION TIME
15 minutes plus 5 minutes
EACH 600 ML
(1 PINT) JUICE
FILLS 2 MEDIUM JARS

Cooking or *eating apples,*
  or *a mixture*
Sugar
Honey
Cloves
A piece of dried ginger root
Cinnamon sticks

(For quantities see method)

BLACKCURRANT AND GERANIUM JELLY

— • —

INGREDIENTS

PREPARATION TIME
5–8 minutes
COOKING TIME
20 minutes
FILLS 4 SMALL JARS

1.5 kg (3 lb) blackcurrants
1 kg (2 ¼ lb) sugar
6 rose-scented geranium
leaves

Blackcurrants are very high in pectin, which is why blackcurrant jam and jelly are so very easy to make – you can always get what the purists call 'a perfect set'. All the same, you may distrust the method I give here – please don't, it makes a perfect jelly, richly flavoured and with just a touch of the lovely scent of rose geranium leaves. This is best kept in the fridge after opening. One of the best jams to serve stirred into chilled yoghurt as an instant dessert. Dilute with warm water to make a syrup for soft-fruit salads, or use it as a glaze over the base of a flan case before filling with other fruit.

Remove the largest stalks from the blackcurrants and put them in the preserving pan with the sugar and the geranium leaves. Cook over a low heat until the juice runs from the fruit and the sugar has melted, then raise the heat and boil fast for 10 minutes. Have a jelly bag ready and tip the contents of the preserving pan, carefully, into it. As soon as all the juice has dripped through, pot the jelly into warmed dry jars. If the juice cools too much while it is going through and begins to set a little, warm it sufficiently to melt it again and to make it easier to pot.

SUMMER BERRY JAM

———— • ————

This jam makes good use of those frozen packs of mixed berries (blackcurrants, raspberries and so on) available in supermarkets, but makes more of them by using apple juice as well. If you are making this in the right season, you might like to use any mixture of summer berries which your greengrocer or supermarket is offering. Do make sure that you use good unsweetened English apple juice, rather than the long-life variety. The end result is a richly flavoured jam which is delicious on scones piled with cream, as the filling of a sponge flan case, topped with whipped cream and fresh fruit, or melted gently, seasoned with a slurp of brandy and used as the sauce for a summer pudding. Try it as a filling for pancakes, too.

———————

Put the fruit and apple juice into a heavy saucepan or preserving pan and bring to a gentle simmer; simmer for 5 minutes, stirring once or twice. Add the sugar and stir while it dissolves, then raise the heat and, when the contents are boiling hard, time for exactly 4 minutes. Draw off the heat and test for setting, then leave for 15 minutes, stir to distribute the fruit and then pot in the warmed, dry jars.

INGREDIENTS

PREPARATION TIME
5 minutes
COOKING TIME
10 minutes
FILLS 4 MEDIUM JARS

1 kg (2 ¼ lb) mixed summer berries
600 ml (1 pint) apple juice
1 kg (2 ¼ lb) sugar-with-pectin

QUICK BRAMBLE JAM

———— • ————

INGREDIENTS

EACH 450 G (1 LB) FRUIT
FILLS 2 MEDIUM JARS

*Equal quantities of
blackberries and
sugar-with-pectin*

You could make this – almost – in time for tea after a blackberrying expedition. Because of its short cooking time, it has the most wonderful fresh flavour, but it also keeps well. One of my favourite jams – piled on to fresh bread spread thickly with butter – it's nothing like so good with low-fat spread. Good in jam tarts, too.

Sort through the blackberries, removing any bits of stalk or leaf, weigh them, rinse them briefly in a colander, then put into a preserving pan with an equal amount of sugar. Bring to boiling point, making sure that the sugar has all melted in the process and the fruit is giving off lots of juice, then boil fast for 3 minutes, stirring well. Pot into warmed, dry jars.

Blackcurrant Mincemeat

— • —

A deliciously different mincemeat which will keep until Christmas, bringing a faint flavour of summer to your mince pies. You can use Honey candied peel (see p. 73) for this recipe, for a truly home-made preserve. It can be used for any recipe where you would use ordinary mincemeat. It makes a good stuffing for baked apples and a spoonful added to a basic apple sauce makes a good accompaniment to roast pork.

Mix all the ingredients, except the brandy, together in a heavy pan and cook over a low heat until the sugar has dissolved. Simmer gently for 20 minutes until the fresh fruit is tender. Remove from the heat, leave to stand for 5 minutes or so and then add the brandy, stirring well. Pot into warm dry jars.

INGREDIENTS

PREPARATION TIME
15 minutes
COOKING TIME
25 minutes
FILLS 4 MEDIUM JARS

450 g (1 lb) blackcurrants, picked from stalks
50 g (2 oz) candied orange peel, finely chopped
4 tart apples, peeled, cored and chopped
100 g (4 oz) raisins
175 g (6 oz) moist brown sugar
50 g (2 oz) skinned and chopped almonds
½ teaspoon ground nutmeg
Juice and grated rind of 1 orange
Juice of 1 lemon
3 tablespoons brandy

DAMSON AND WALNUT JAM

— • —

INGREDIENTS

PREPARATION TIME
15 minutes
COOKING TIME
25 minutes
FILLS 4 MEDIUM JARS

900 g (2 lb) damsons
1.2 litres (2 pints) water
2 generous sprigs fresh
rosemary
900 g (2 lb) sugar-with-
pectin
175–200 g (6–7 oz)
walnut pieces

Again, this jam is made with the addition of herbs, in the French manner. Don't use too much rosemary, as you don't want its flavour to dominate – you can omit it altogether if you prefer. The walnuts add texture and a warm nutty flavour to this rich autumn preserve. If you can buy the fresh walnuts which appear in this country about September, and can be bothered to crack them, and peel off the bitter inner skin, they are perfect for this jam. If not, use ordinary walnut pieces, but check the sell-by date on the packet as they can go rancid. This is a perfect jam to spread on hot buttered crumpets or muffins.

Put the damsons, water and rosemary into a heavy pan and simmer gently until soft. Remove the rosemary and push the fruit and its juice through a food mill or sieve, taking out the stones as they appear – this is fiddly and messy but much quicker and easier than removing the stones from the raw fruit. Put the pulp into a preserving pan with the sugar, bring slowly to the boil and then boil hard for 2 minutes. Add the walnut pieces at this point, then boil for a further 1½–2 minutes or until setting point is reached. Pot into warm, dry jars.

DAMSON
CHEESE

—— • ——

You can use this basic method to make damson cheese, using double quantities and omitting the walnuts. Keep the jam at a steady simmer rather than a boil, stirring frequently, until it is so thick that a wooden spoon drawn through it will leave the base of the pan clean. This will take some time. Pot the cheese in warm, dry straight-sided jars, which should be lightly oiled with a flavourless oil such as almond. This will allow you to turn out the cheese in order to slice it. This will keep for years if well covered. Serve the damson cheese with Stilton at Christmas, or with cold meat.

CRYSTALLIZED FLOWERS

——— • ———

INGREDIENTS

PREPARATION TIME
*Overnight for the
gum to dissolve*

*25 g (1 oz) gum arabic
About 2 tablespoons rose-
or orange flower water
Caster or granulated sugar
Suitable flowers or leaves*

My mother used to decorate our birthday cakes with the crystallized flowers of the season – primroses for me, wild roses for my sister – one of the treats was being able to eat the sweet and crunchy decorations. They are very easy to do, but shouldn't be made at the last minute as they do need a period of time to dry out. Mrs Beeton gives details for crystallizing holly leaves, too, which make unusual and very successful decorations for Christmas cakes, although they shouldn't be eaten. Avoid also poisonous flowers such as laburnum or foxgloves. Edible gum arabic can be bought from cake decoration specialists. Simply shaped flowers and leaves are best. Caster sugar is best for flowers, but the coarser crystals of granulated sugar are effective for leaves as they catch the light – particularly suitable for those Christmas holly leaves. Use rose petals to decorate a strawberry filled cake or flan, or pot marigolds to add colour to a cheesecake, or arrange crystallized primroses in the centre of a Simnel cake.

Put the gum arabic into a small screw-top jar and cover completely with rose- or orange flower water. Leave in a warm place overnight, until the gum has completely dissolved. Sift a little sugar on to a plate and have a cake-rack spread with a sheet of baking parchment ready. Using an ordinary paintbrush, paint the flower carefully with the gum solution, covering both sides of the petals, then dip briefly and lightly in the sugar, gently shaking off any surplus. Put each flower or leaf as it is done on the cake rack to dry. When you have done as many as you want, transfer the cake rack to the airing cupboard and leave the flowers to set for a minimum of an hour. They can then be used at once or packed between layers of baking parchment in a plastic box, to keep until required.

CHERRIES IN WINE

— • —

The cherry season, for our own English cherries, is short and so there have to be extra special ways of extending it. This recipe comes from France where they use herbs with fruit in very interesting ways; the fresh bay leaves called for here add a slight flavour of almonds to the syrup. They should be available from most supermarkets but if you can't find them use 1 dried bay leaf instead.

This is a very versatile preserve, useful for both savoury and sweet dishes. Serve very cold with *crème fraîche* as an instant dessert, or use the fruit for a clafoutis (baked batter pudding), reducing the syrup to use as a sauce. Use to make a sauce for roast duck, or venison. Braise pigeons in the syrup and add a few of the cherries at the last minute.

Wash the fruit and drain between paper towels. Pull off the stalks but don't stone the fruit. Bring the wine, sugar and bay leaves to a boil, lower the heat and simmer until syrupy – about 10 minutes. Add the fruit and simmer very gently for another 10 minutes until the cherries are just tender. Remove the bay leaves and pour syrup and fruit into the clean, dry and warmed jar.

INGREDIENTS

PREPARATION TIME
5–7 minutes
COOKING TIME
20 minutes
FILLS 1 LARGE
PRESERVING JAR

900 g (2 lb) fresh cherries
600 ml (1 pint) full-bodied red wine
225 g (8 oz) granulated sugar
2 fresh bay leaves or 1 dried

LIME CURD

— • —

PREPARATION TIME
10 minutes
COOKING TIME
20 minutes
FILLS 3 SMALL JARS

4 limes
5 eggs, beaten
100g (4 oz) unsalted
butter, diced
350g (12 oz) caster sugar

This is just as rich and delicious as lemon curd, but the limes add an extra aromatic flavour. During the Seville orange season in January this can be made with the grated rind and juice of 3 small marmalade oranges instead. It can also be made in the microwave. Lime curd makes a delicious filling for tartlets made with an almond pastry – try decorating each with a small piece of crystallized ginger. Or stir into whipped cream and use to fill brandy snaps. Use Seville orange curd to fill a chocolate roulade, or to sandwich a lemon sponge cake.

Scrub the limes, dry them, then grate the rind and squeeze the juice into a bowl which will fit neatly and firmly over a medium-sized saucepan without touching the bottom of the pan. Pour in the beaten eggs through a sieve to catch the lumpy bits, then add the diced butter and the sugar. Put the bowl over the pan half filled with hot, not boiling, water and stir constantly. As the butter and sugar melt and amalgamate with the eggs, the mixture will slowly thicken until it becomes the consistency of thick cream, which will take about 20 minutes. To make the curd in the microwave, put the butter into a microwavable bowl and microwave on HIGH for about 1 minute. Add the remaining ingredients and cook on HIGH for 3½–4 minutes, stirring 3 times, by which time the sugar should have dissolved. Cook on HIGH for another 3½–4 minutes or until the mixture thickens, stirring every half minute or so to stop the mixture curdling. Pot into clean, dry jars. Keep in the fridge after opening.

FREEZER JAMS

—— • ——

There are times, when there is a glut of fruit and life is particularly hectic when even the fastest jam takes too much time and effort. This is where freezer jams come in. Pot these in small quantities, keep in the freezer and use as you might a cooked jam. As these are made with raw fruit the flavour captures all the magic of summer, especially as it is the soft fruit that responds best to this treatment – raspberries, strawberries and, best of all, if you can get them, mulberries. You can use single types of fruit or a mixture – whatever is available. Use freezer jams for sorbets, ices, to fill meringues, to heat and pour over steamed puddings, or just to eat with plain yoghurt as an instant dessert.

———

Hull strawberries, otherwise just mix the fruit thoroughly with the sugar in a large bowl and leave overnight. Next day, purée the fruit in batches in a food processor or blender, return to the bowl and stir the strained lemon juice into the purée before spooning into clean yoghurt cartons or other small containers with lids. I find freezing the jam in 100 g (4 oz) and 225 g (8 oz) portions most useful – allowing a space for the jam to expand as it freezes.

To use, remove from the freezer and allow to defrost. Once thawed, it will keep in the fridge for about a week because of the high sugar content.

INGREDIENTS

PREPARATION TIME
5 minutes plus overnight

1.75 kg (4 lb) soft fruit
900 g (2 lb) caster sugar
Juice of 2 lemons

*E*LIZA ACTON'S
GROSEILLÉE

—— • ——

INGREDIENTS

PREPARATION TIME
15 minutes
COOKING TIME
20–25 minutes
FILLS 5 MEDIUM JARS

900 g (2 lb) ripe gooseberries, topped and tailed
750 g (1 ½ lb) raspberries
About 1.5 kg (3 lb) sugar-with-pectin

Eliza Acton's *Modern Cookery in all its Branches* was first published in 1845, and was subtitled *reduced to a System of Easy Practice*. Her recipe for mixed gooseberry and raspberry jam is typical of her quicker and easier methods. She first gives the lengthier version, cooking both fruits separately and then combining them, and then adds a note to say that 'When more convenient, a portion of the raspberries can be boiled with the gooseberries at first'. It makes a better jam, too, I think. I also feel that she would have taken advantage of using sugar-with-pectin, as the reduced cooking time contributes greatly to capturing the flavour of the fresh fruit. A good jam for using with cakes – to sandwich a Victoria sponge, to spread over a Swiss roll before it is rolled, and so on. Keep in the fridge once opened.

Cook the fruit together gently, without water, until soft (this can be done in a low oven, or in the microwave). Push through a food mill or sieve. Weigh the purée and return it to the pan with an equal amount of sugar. Bring slowly to the boil, then boil hard for about 3½ minutes before testing for setting (see p. 10). Stir this jam frequently to prevent it burning. Pot into warm, dry jars.

KUMQUATS IN
BRANDY SYRUP

—— • ——

The surprising thing about kumquats, the smallest of all the citrus fruits, is that it is the peel that is sweet while the flesh is very tart. This recipe is very easy to do, is a wonderful standby preserve and one which makes a delicious and good-looking present. It also makes a wonderful accompaniment to rich chocolate desserts, and ice-cream. Any remaining syrup makes a good syllabub, or can be warmed and poured over a freshly baked orange sponge cake.

———

Wash and halve the kumquats, discarding any pips. Dissolve the sugar in the water over a low heat, raise the heat until the mixture boils, add the fruit and lower the heat to a simmer. Cook for about 25 minutes, until the kumquat skins can be pierced easily with a skewer. Lift out the fruit with a draining spoon and place in the warm, dry jars. The syrup should be thick enough to pour straight over the fruit – if it needs thickening a little more, simmer for a further 5 minutes before adding to the fruit in the jar. Top up the jars with the brandy, cap tightly and store in a cool place, shaking the jars from time to time. This can be eaten straight away, but is best kept for a week first.

INGREDIENTS

PREPARATION TIME
5 minutes
COOKING TIME
30 minutes
FILLS 2 MEDIUM JARS

450 g (1 lb) kumquats
175 g (6 oz) granulated sugar
300 ml (10 fl oz) water
About 150 ml (5 fl oz) brandy

SEVILLE ORANGE JELLY

—— • ——

INGREDIENTS

PREPARATION TIME
5 minutes plus overnight
COOKING TIME
21 minutes
FILLS 4 MEDIUM JARS

6 Seville oranges
1.2 litres (2 pints) water
About 900 g (2 lb)
  sugar-with-pectin

As a child I used to love the taste of my mother's bitter orange marmalade but hated the peel and so for my own satisfaction I invented this recipe, made all the easier since the advent of sugar-with-pectin. It has a lovely brisk, fresh, light flavour, perfect for breakfast. If you do not have a pressure cooker in which to cook the oranges, leave them to cook all day in a very low oven if that is more convenient than cooking them on the hob. This jelly is delicious with toasted brown muffins and lots of butter and there are those who like it with crisply fried bacon. Makes a good glaze for roast pork and ham. Add a spoonful stirred into jugged hare.

Scrub the oranges and cut them into rough chunks. Put them in the pressure cooker with the water, bring to full pressure and cook for 20 minutes. Reduce pressure slowly. Tip the contents of the pressure cooker into a jelly bag, suspend over a bowl and leave to drip for at least 3 hours, or overnight in a cool place if you prefer. Then measure the liquid and allow 450 g (1 lb) sugar-with-pectin for each 600 ml (1 pint) juice. Put into a preserving pan, bring to a full boil and boil fast for 1 minute. Test for setting (see p. 10) and check after each half-minute interval. Pot into warmed, dry jars.

PRESERVED NECTARINES

—— • ——

Nectarines become very cheap late in the summer and it is worth preserving a reasonable quantity then to put aside for Christmas presents. You can get away with an undistinguished white wine here, especially if you chose to add the rose-scented geranium or lemon balm leaves. Use wide-mouthed preserving jars to make it easier to extract the fruit. You can serve these just as they are, lightly chilled and topped with toasted flaked almonds, or you can use them to decorate and fill a hazelnut sponge, or a pavlova. Add sliced strawberries and some raspberries to make a fruit salad.

———

Bring the wine, sugar and leaves (if using) to a gentle simmer and cook over a low heat for 15 minutes. Meanwhile, dip each nectarine into a pan of simmering water, using a skewer or carving fork. Hold in the water for a slow count of 20, by which time the skin should be able to be slipped off. Halve the fruit and remove the stone. Poach gently in the wine syrup for 10 minutes, then pack the nectarines carefully into the clean, dry jars. Boil up the syrup for another minute, remove the leaves, and pour over the fruit. Clip on the lids at once.

INGREDIENTS

PREPARATION TIME
20 minutes
COOKING TIME
25 minutes
FILLS 2 LARGE OR 4
SMALL PRESERVING JARS

12 nectarines
900 ml (1 ½ pints) white wine
350 g (12 oz) granulated sugar
A small bunch of rose geranium or *lemon balm leaves (optional)*

SUPERFAST PEACH AND APRICOT PRESERVE

—— • ——

INGREDIENTS

PREPARATION TIME
5 minutes
COOKING TIME
20 minutes
FILLS 4 MEDIUM JARS

1 × 411 g (14½ oz) can apricot halves in fruit juice
1 × 411 g (14½ oz) can peach slices in fruit juice
825 g (1 lb 13 oz) sugar-with-pectin
Grated rind of 1 lemon and the juice of ½ lemon

This recipe cheats brazenly, making use of the excellent quality tinned fruit around, but it has such a good flavour that you could give a jar to the most experienced jam-maker you know without a blush. It is also extremely popular, I'm told, with teenage boys. Make sure you buy fruit canned in fruit juice, rather than syrup, and experiment with other fruits and flavourings, such as black cherries with cinnamon, or pineapple with grated lime rind and juice. Serve this with warmed croissants or brioches for breakfast or brunch.

Process the contents of the tins briefly in the food processor so that you have a chunky purée. In a preserving pan mix the sugar with this purée, add the grated lemon rind and juice. Dissolve the sugar over a low heat, then bring to a full rolling boil. Boil for exactly 4 minutes, test for setting (see p. 10). Leave the jam to settle for 15 minutes, then stir before potting to distribute the fruit. Pot into warm dry jars.

Opposite: KUMQUATS IN BRANDY SYRUP (*page 63*)
QUICK BRAMBLE JAM (*page 54*)

Overleaf: STRAWBERRY AND REDCURRANT PRESERVE (*page 76*)
PRESERVED NECTARINES (*page 65*)

RUBY ORANGE
MARMALADE

—— • ——

The season for ruby, or blood oranges as they are also known, is as fleeting as that for Seville oranges so it is good to have a recipe that preserves their uniquely sharp strawberryish flavour. This one does as it needs to be cooked for such a short time after the sugar is added; a pressure cooker is a great help here too. The colour takes some getting used to as a breakfast preserve, but don't be put off. You can use the same method for a clementine or tangerine marmalade.

This can accompany anything chocolatey; try spreading a spoonful over the base of each ramekin before pouring in a dark chocolate mousse mixture. Use to spread over a chocolate roulade before spreading with cream and rolling it up. Use as the basis of a sauce for sautéed duck breasts, or add a spoonful to Cumbrian sauce (see p. 31) instead of using rowan or redcurrant jelly.

———

Scrub the oranges thoroughly, cut in half lengthways then slice finely, removing any pips you come across. Put into the pressure cooker with the water, bring to full pressure then cook for 12 minutes. Reduce pressure quickly and test to see that the peel is quite soft. Tip in the sugar, stir well and set the open pressure cooker pan over a moderate heat. Bring to a full boil and boil fast for 4 minutes. Remove from the heat, let it stand for about 15 minutes before potting so that the peel doesn't rise to the surface of the jars.

If not using a pressure cooker, simmer the orange slices for about 45 minutes (using an extra 300 ml (10 fl oz) water to allow for evaporation) before adding the sugar.

Preceding page: SALMON CURED IN VODKA AND LIME

(*page 85*)

Opposite: POTTED HERB CHEESE (*page 93*)

INGREDIENTS

PREPARATION TIME
15 minutes
COOKING TIME
35 minutes
FILLS 3–4 MEDIUM JARS

750 g (1 ½ lb) blood oranges
600 ml (1 pint) water
750 g (1 ½ lb) sugar-with-pectin

FRAGRANT PRUNES

— • —

INGREDIENTS

PREPARATION TIME
10 minutes
COOKING TIME
15 minutes
WAITING TIME
1 month
FILLS 1 LARGE
PRESERVING JAR

450 g (1 lb) prunes
600 ml (1 pint) freshly
brewed Earl Grey tea
100 g (4 oz) clear honey
150 ml (5 fl oz) rum

This is an interesting treatment for prunes, rendering them subtle and glamorous with very little effort. You can use any of the varieties of dried prune; the very best of all are those which can be found in markets in the Agen region of France in mid-September. These might be described as *demi-sec*, midway between plum and prune, and are worth bringing home for this recipe. Serve these, chilled, with sweet crisp biscuits, as an instant dessert. Or use some of the slightly diluted juice to deglaze the pan after frying pork steaks, adding some of the chopped prunes as well. Or you can use both fruit and syrup as the basis for a winter fruit salad, adding any ready-to-eat dried fruit you choose and making up more tea and honey syrup as required.

Pack the prunes into a clean dry preserving jar. Strain the tea into a pan, stir in the honey and bring to the boil over a medium heat. Simmer steadily until syrupy – about 15 minutes. Pour this hot mixture over the prunes and leave until cold. Top up the jar with the rum. Clip on the lid and leave in a cool dark place for at least a month before eating, shaking the jar occasionally.

HONEY CANDIED PEEL

— • —

I was given this idea by a beekeeper at a local food fair, as she sold me a jar of her own peel in honey. This is a delicious preserve, to be used in the same way as candied peel in cakes and biscuits. I like to make it in the winter with tangerine and clementine peel, saving the discarded peel in a plastic bag in the fridge until I have enough to fill a jar. It is much nicer than commercial candied peel for almost anything you can think of. It makes a very good stuffing for ordinary baked apples, combined with dried fruit, and a spoonful is excellent stirred into the fruit for any crumble or pie.

Cut the peel into neat pieces – squares or strips – and blanch it in boiling water for 5 minutes. Drain and refresh in cold water, then pat dry on paper towels. Put a layer into a clean dry jar, cover with a tablespoonful of runny honey, add another layer of peel and another of honey, until you have used up all the peel. Cap the jar tightly and leave in a cool place, but not too far out of sight as you will need to shake the jar from time to time, and to check that the top layer of peel is still covered with honey. If it isn't, add some more. And you can add more peel to the jar, blanching it first, whenever you have some. After about 3 months, it should be ready for use. I think it improves with age, too, as long as you don't let it dry out.

INGREDIENTS

PREPARATION TIME
5 minutes
COOKING TIME
5 minutes
WAITING TIME
3 months

100–175 g (4–6 oz) citrus peel
450 g (1 lb) runny honey

SUPERFINE RASPBERRY JAM

—— • ——

INGREDIENTS

PREPARATION TIME
1 minute
COOKING TIME
20 minutes
EACH 450 G (1 LB) FRUIT
FILLS 2 SMALL JARS

About 1 kg (2 ¼ lb)
 raspberries
About 1.25 kg (2 ¾ lb)
 sugar

This has always been my favourite raspberry jam re-cipe, as it is simplicity itself and captures all the flavour of the fruit. And it keeps surprisingly well – at least a year in my experience, and longer, I'm told by the friend who also loves this recipe. For the very best flavour, make this as soon as possible after the fruit has been picked, preferably on a dry day, but if buying them ready-picked, check for freshness, firmness and lack of mould. This jam is best used when it can exhibit that flavour to the full – spoon it over fresh sliced nectarines or peaches, or over good quality vanilla ice-cream (or both together, to make Nectarine or Peach Melba).

Pre-heat the oven to gas mark 4, 350°F (180°C). Weigh your raspberries into a large ovenproof bowl and then weigh an equal quantity plus 225 g (8 oz) of sugar into another large ovenproof bowl. Put both bowls into the oven for about 20 minutes or until both raspberries and sugar are perfectly hot. Then quickly and thoroughly mix the fruit with the sugar and pot into warmed dry jars.

CHRISTMAS RAISINS

——— • ———

For this Christmas delicacy you must have the best possible quality raisins, often to be found in good health-food shops rather than supermarkets. This is not unlike a high-class and very alcoholic mincemeat – make it in October to have it ready for Christmas as it makes a very good present for consenting adults. You can remove the raisins from the syrup and spread on a plate to serve with nuts as part of a winter dessert. Add them to apple pies, or to make a spicy wintery ice-cream or syllabub.

Make a syrup with the sugar, water, the rind and juice of the orange and lemon and simmer for 5 minutes. Add the raisins and simmer for another 10, until they have plumped up. Cool, then add the rum and pot into the clean, dry jar. Shake the jar from time to time. Decant into smaller jars, if preferred, to give as presents.

INGREDIENTS

PREPARATION TIME
5 minutes
COOKING TIME
15 minutes
FILLS 1 MEDIUM
PRESERVING JAR

450 g (1 lb) muscovado sugar
300 ml (10 fl oz) water
Juice and grated rind of 1 orange
Juice and grated rind of 1 lemon
450 g (1 lb) best raisins, stoned
150 ml (5 fl oz) rum

STRAWBERRY AND REDCURRANT PRESERVE

——— • ———

INGREDIENTS

PREPARATION TIME
15–20 minutes plus overnight
COOKING TIME
35 minutes
FILLS 4–5 MEDIUM JARS

900 g (2 lb) redcurrants
900 ml (1 ½ pints) water
750 g (1 ½ lb) preserving sugar
750 g (1 ½ lb) strawberries

This is an old recipe, which results in the whole strawberries being suspended in the redcurrant jelly. It isn't the fastest way I know of making strawberry jam, but it is one of the best and it really doesn't take much extra effort. It should have a soft set. Try spooning this jam over fresh sliced strawberries and whipped cream in a flan case, rather than using sugar. You can make it even more special by adding rose-water, to taste, just before potting.

Remove the largest stalks from the redcurrants (no need to get rid of all the tiny ones), put them in a pan with the water and simmer for about 15–20 minutes until the fruit is well softened. Then tip the contents of the pan into a jelly bag and allow to drip overnight. Next day, measure the juice, which should be 900 ml (1½ pints), into a preserving pan, add the sugar and set to melt over a low heat. Hull the strawberries and, if they are large, halve or even quarter them, then add them to the juice and sugar in the pan. Bring to a full rolling boil and boil hard for 4–5 minutes, until setting point is reached (see p. 10). Leave to stand for 15 minutes before potting, and stir to distribute the fruit, then pot into the warmed, dry jars.

RHUBARB, ORANGE AND GINGER JAM

— • —

This is a most delicious jam, good to make in early summer when the rhubarb stalks are thick and green and much fuller of sugar than when young and pink. This recipe adds the classic flavourings of orange and ginger, but with a sophisticated difference – small chunks of crystallized ginger. This jam is very good used for a pudding taught me by a Swiss friend. Trim medium-thick slices of white bread and fry until crisp in butter. Drain on paper towels and leave to cool on a cake rack. Just before serving, spread thickly with the jam and serve with cream.

Wash and trim the rhubarb and cut into 3 cm (1 inch) pieces. Put them into a large bowl with the juice and grated rind of the oranges, and the sugar. Mix all together thoroughly, then leave overnight. Next day, tip the contents of the bowl into a preserving pan together with the ginger root, or the freeze-dried ginger in a spice ball or muslin bag. Set over a low heat and cook gently until the rhubarb has softened – about 10 minutes. Then raise the heat and bring to a full boil. Boil hard for 4 minutes, then test for setting point (see p. 10). Remove the root ginger and add the crystallized ginger, stir well and leave the jam to stand for a further 15 minutes or so, then stir again just before potting to distribute the ginger throughout the jam. Pot into warm, dry jars.

INGREDIENTS

PREPARATION TIME
10–15 minutes plus overnight
COOKING TIME
30 minutes
FILLS 4 MEDIUM JARS

900 g (2 lb) rhubarb stalks
Juice and grated rind of 2 large juicy oranges
900 g (2 lb) sugar-with-pectin
1 teaspoon freeze-dried ginger or a piece of dried root ginger, lightly bruised
50–75 g (2–3 oz) finely chopped crystallized ginger

TOMATO JAM

INGREDIENTS

PREPARATION TIME
5 minutes
COOKING TIME
15 minutes
FILLS 4 SMALL JARS

2 × 400 g (14 oz) cans
chopped tomatoes
300 ml (10 fl oz)
unsweetened orange juice
1 vanilla pod
Rind of 1 lemon
About 750 g (1 ½ lb)
sugar-with-pectin

I always regarded it as odd, having been brought up in the English tradition to think of the tomato as a vegetable rather than a fruit, to hear my mother-in-law reminiscing about giving her children sliced tomatoes sprinkled with sugar and served with cream. Some people dislike the idea of tomato *jam*, but try it, it has a delicious and subtle flavour. But don't attempt it with fresh tomatoes unless you are sure that those you have available really do have masses of flavour. Use this jam to sandwich a walnut cake, or to spread on plain scones. It is also good added in small quantities to bitter salads of chicory and radicchio and to tomato sauces and soups. Delicious with cheese or olive breads. Mix with a little sherry vinegar and olive oil to dress vegetable salads. Mix with a few drops of Tabasco and some Worcestershire sauce to use as a barbecue marinade.

Tip the tomatoes into a measuring jug to check their liquid quantity, then put into a preserving pan together with the orange juice, vanilla pod and the lemon rind. Stir well and simmer gently for 10 minutes. Add 450 g (1 lb) sugar for each 600 ml (1 pint) of chopped tomato. Bring to the boil and boil for 4 minutes, testing for setting point (see p. 10) – this is a jam which is all the better for a light set. Fish out the lemon rind and vanilla pod and pot the jam into warm, dry jars.

POTTING AND CURING

No well-stocked larder, before the advent of the deep-freeze, would be without a brine tub in which joints of beef and pork gradually absorbed the salt which would preserve them, or without little pots of savoury pastes, making economical use of left-over meat and game, that would grace tea and breakfast tables.

Such dishes might at first glance seem time-consuming to prepare, but, as Eliza Acton said of bread-making, the time they take isn't *your* time – Spiced beef (see p. 88) needs a minute's attention daily for a week, cooks slowly without any attention, and then provides several good meals. What more could you ask?

To help preserve potted meats and fish, it is important to drain them of any cooking juices first, and also to seal them with clarified butter. (To make this, see the recipes for Spiced clarified butter on p. 98, omitting the spices.) In this way they will keep for up to a fortnight in the fridge, although once the butter seal has been broken they should be eaten within 24 hours. Bacteria-slaughtering saltpetre was a far more necessary ingredient in the days when the production of meat was less hygienic than it is now, and when the salting process had to preserve meat for months on end. Now it is no longer necessary – salting is much more of a cosmetic process these days, providing a delicious alternative to fresh meat rather than a vital method of preservation – which is just as well as saltpetre is so hard to obtain. The reason for this is that it is actually potassium nitrate and an ingredient of explosives. I experimented without and found that it made no difference to the finished product except to the colour of the meat, which was a little less luridly pink.

Perhaps the best thing about all the recipes in this chapter is that they are meals in themselves, and therefore endlessly useful to have in the larder or fridge for packed lunches, high teas, late suppers, even breakfasts. These are the original convenience foods and deserve a revival.

COD'S ROE PASTE

PREPARATION TIME
10 minutes

175 g (6 oz) cooked cod's roe
1–2 teaspoons Dijon mustard
Salt and freshly ground black pepper
Squeeze of lemon juice
75 g (3 oz) salted butter, melted

This is a delicious paste to make when the fishmonger has fresh, cooked (not smoked) cod's roe on his slab – you could call it the English equivalent of taramasalata. Since cod became more expensive so has its roe, but this makes economical use of it. This is a perfect late-night snack, as well as making a good starter. It is lovely on hot buttered toast or crumpets for a winter tea.

Scrape the cooked roe away from the skin and put it in a blender or food processor, together with 1 teaspoon of mustard, salt, a generous grinding of pepper and the lemon juice. Process until well blended, then taste and see if you want that other teaspoonful of mustard. I like quite a lot myself. If so, add it and process again to blend it in. Taste again to check the seasoning, then spoon the mixture into small clean pots and top with the melted butter. This will keep for a week in the fridge, but once you have broken the seal of butter, eat within 24 hours.

KARIN PERRY'S GRAVLAX

—— • ——

Karin Perry and I wrote together for several years for the *Sunday Telegraph* and this is her recipe for this classic Swedish dish, which appears in her excellent *The Fish Book*. She makes the valuable point that, if you are worried about eating raw fish, freezing the fish for three days beforehand will kill any parasite. If you do decide to do this, make sure the fish has thawed thoroughly before giving it the curing treatment.

Make sure that there are no bones left in the salmon fillets, and scrape the skin side with a sharp knife, away from you, to remove any stray scales. Mix together the sugar, salt, and pepper and sprinkle over the salmon flesh, rubbing it in well. Spread some of the dill over the bottom of a shallow dish and put in one of the fillets, skin side down; cover with more dill. Put the remaining fillet on top of the first, skin side up and spread more dill over the top. Cover with a piece of foil, then a plate of similar size to the fish and weight it and put in the fridge. Turn the fish every 12 hours and spoon over it the salty juices which will have gathered in the dish. It will be ready to eat after 2 days, but will keep for 4. Scrape off most of the dill, then slice the fish thinly at an angle ready to serve. Then make the sauce: mix together the mustard, sugar, dill, vinegar and salt and pepper. Then whisk in the oil. Serve with the sliced salmon.

INGREDIENTS

PREPARATION TIME
15–20 minutes
CURING TIME
2 days

1 kg (2 ¼ lb) middle cut of salmon, filleted but with the skin on
1 ½ tablespoons sugar
2 tablespoons salt
1 teaspoon crushed black peppercorns
About 4 tablespoons coarsely chopped fresh dill

FOR THE SAUCE
2 tablespoons mild mustard
1 teaspoon sugar
1 tablespoon finely chopped fresh dill
2 teaspoons white wine vinegar
Salt and freshly ground black pepper
150 ml (5 fl oz) grapeseed oil

ROLLMOP HERRINGS

— • —

INGREDIENTS

PREPARATION TIME
15 minutes
WAITING TIME
5 days

450 ml (15 fl oz) white
  wine vinegar
150 ml (5 fl oz) water
1 tablespoon salt
2 teaspoons caraway or
  mustard seeds
8 herrings, cleaned and
  split
8 small pickled cucumbers
  or gherkins
1 small onion, thinly sliced
2 fresh or dried red chillies
2 bay leaves
3 blades mace

S omeone once gave me his definition of a poorly made rollmop herring as being like 'an old face flannel in battery acid' and I have tasted versions that do fulfil that description. This recipe does, I hope, produce something better. You can keep a jar of these for some time in the fridge, ready to have on hand for a quick starter, or to serve as part of a mixed hors d'oeuvre. To accompany the rollmops, try blending 150 ml (5 fl oz) soured cream or fromage frais with 2 tablespoons of Nerine's quicker pickled beetroot (p. 23) or Pen-friend's pickled cabbage (p. 25). Either of these will set off the sharp vinegary flavour of the fish. Serve with slices of buttered rye bread.

———

Bring the vinegar and water to the boil, together with the salt and the mustard or caraway seeds, then leave to cool while you prepare the herrings. Wrap each herring, skin side outside, round a pickled cucumber or gherkin and pin in place with a wooden cocktail stick (these have the added advantage of making the rollmops easier to get out of the jar). Arrange them in a large, clean glass preserving jar, adding rings of the onion as you do so, and pushing the chillies, bay leaves and mace down amongst them. Pour the cooled vinegar over them, making sure they are completely covered, then cover and store in the fridge. Keep for about 5 days before eating; they will last for about 3 weeks in the fridge.

SOUSED MACKEREL

—— • ——

The long, slow cooking of this dish, in a mildly spiced vinegar *court bouillon*, renders the fish digestible and delicious, the bones become as soft as those in tinned sardines so it is popular with those who normally fear bones. It works just as well with herrings, but both fish should be cleaned, the herring split and the mackerel filleted. A good fishmonger will be happy to do this, or you can buy these ready-prepared and pre-packed in many supermarkets. Soused mackerel is at its best about 3 days after making, and will keep for up to a week in the fridge. Delicious eaten chilled, with brown bread and butter and some mayonnaise which you have flavoured with a spoonful or two of the Raw apple chutney found on p. 20.

———

Pre-heat the oven to gas mark 1, 275°F (140°C). Arrange the mackerel in a shallow ovenproof dish and cover with the sliced onion, bay leaves, peppercorns and mace. Sprinkle with the salt. Mix the wine, vinegar and water and pour into the dish. The fish should be covered by the liquid, if not add more of any one of the liquid ingredients according to your taste. Cover with a lid, or a piece of foil, and cook in the oven for 2½–3 hours. When the mackerel are cooked, transfer them to another shallow dish and strain their cooking liquid over them, then cool and store in the fridge.

INGREDIENTS

PREPARATION TIME
10 minutes
COOKING TIME
2½–3 hours
WAITING TIME
3 days

2 large mackerel, filleted
1 small onion, sliced
2 bay leaves
6 black peppercorns
2 blades mace
1 teaspoon salt
300 ml (10 fl oz) white wine
300 ml (10 fl oz) white wine vinegar
300 ml (10 fl oz) water

SMOKED HADDOCK PASTE

— • —

PREPARATION TIME
15–20 minutes
COOKING TIME
15 minutes

*225 g (8 oz) cooked
smoked haddock*
*100 g (4 oz) unsalted
butter, softened, plus
75 g (3 oz) extra for
sealing*
A pinch of cayenne
½ teaspoon ground mace

I prefer this paste to any other made with smoked fish –
the butter content blends beautifully with the smoky
flavour and firm but not oily texture of the fish. Use
undyed fish if possible – not only is the colour less hectic,
but the flavour is better too. Serve a ramekin of this,
together with thin slices of crisp brown toast and lemon
quarters, as an easy first course for a picnic dinner. For a
simple lunch or supper, fork generous chunks of this
paste into split baked potatoes and serve with a water-
cress salad.

Make sure that all skin and bones have been removed
from the haddock, and that it is well drained of its juices.
Put it in a blender or food processor with the butter and
blend or process until smooth. Add the seasonings to
taste – much will depend on how salty the fish was in the
first place, but you shouldn't need any more salt. Pack the
paste into small clean pots and seal with a thin layer of
melted butter.

SALMON CURED IN VODKA AND LIME

—— • ——

This recipe makes use of both the alcohol and the acid in the lime to 'cook' the fish and to 'cure' it at the same time. You can keep the fish in its curing marinade for up to seven days in the fridge. The flavours are perfect for light summer meals. If you can't get lemon thyme, don't be tempted to use ordinary thyme as it has such a different type of flavour; better to use the finely grated zest of the lime, and a fresh bay leaf, instead. To serve, slice as thinly, on the slant, as possible and arrange on a bed of thinly sliced avocado and Little Gem lettuce dressed with a lime juice and grapeseed oil dressing.

Make sure that all the tiny bones have been removed from the salmon, and that the skin is free from scales. (Scrape the skin side with a sharp knife, away from you, to remove any stray scale.) Mix the vodka, lime juice, sugar, salt and crushed peppercorns together, then strip the leaves from the lemon thyme and add them. Spoon some of this mixture over the flesh side of the salmon fillets and rub well in, then put the fillets flesh side down in a shallow dish in a single layer and pour the rest of the marinade over them. Cover with foil or cling film and leave for at least 24 hours – basting once or twice with the marinade – or up to a week, basting daily.

INGREDIENTS

PREPARATION TIME
5–10 minutes
CURING TIME
24 hours–7 days

450 g (1 lb) middle cut of salmon, filleted but with the skin on
5 tablespoons vodka
1 tablespoon freshly squeezed lime juice
A pinch of sugar
2 teaspoons sea salt
1 teaspoon green peppercorns, crushed
A generous sprig of lemon thyme

POTTED SHRIMPS

—— • ——

INGREDIENTS

PREPARATION TIME
5 minutes
COOKING TIME
10 minutes

175 g (6 oz) salted butter
1 teaspoon ground mace
A grating of nutmeg
450 g (1 lb) cooked and
shelled shrimps
Salt
A few drops of Tabasco
Bay leaves

An all-time favourite and a classic way to start a typically English meal or to serve at a high tea. You really should have small brown shrimps for this, but if you can't get them, use the larger pink ones, ready cooked. These will keep for some time in the fridge under their layer of air-excluding butter and you can freeze them if necessary but remember to wrap them well so that the butter doesn't pick up any off flavours in the freezer, which it is apt to do. Potted shrimps are best served chilled, with brown bread and butter and lemon quarters, but they can make really special sandwiches – thinly butter slices of brown bread, cover with slices of smoked salmon sprinkled with black pepper and lemon juice, then add a spoonful of potted shrimps as a filling. Partner with quartered hearts of Little Gem lettuce.

Over a low heat, melt 150 g (5 oz) of the butter in a heavy pan, together with the mace and nutmeg (add the latter to taste, not forgetting that nutmeg has a slightly anaesthetizing effect on the taste-buds if used too generously). Add the shrimps and stir well to mix with the spicy butter. Put a lid on the pan and allow the shrimps to soak up the butter over minimal heat for 10 minutes. Add salt to taste, depending on how salty the shrimps were, and a drop or two of Tabasco. Put into small, clean pots and cool. Melt the final 25 g (1 oz) butter and pour it over the top of the shrimps to seal, and press a bay leaf into the soft butter as a finishing touch.

POTTED TROUT

—— • ——

Potted fish was frequently set to bake in the oven as it cooled after bread-making without any liquid, but with quantities of butter – the finished dish consisting of the cooked fish set in its cooking butter. I have developed a rather less rich modern version which adds the flavour of thyme to farmed rainbow trout and uses a quarter of the amount of butter. You can use either whole trout or trout fillets for this recipe – the former are cheaper but take a fraction longer to prepare, the latter are quicker and there is no waste. Again, like Potted shrimps (p. 86), potted trout makes good sandwiches. It's also very good added to kedgeree, or melting over a plate of pasta.

Season the fish with salt, pepper and the lemon juice, then arrange them in a steamer. Fill the bottom of the steamer with well-salted water to which you add the thyme and then steam the fish until the flesh flakes easily with the point of a knife. Whole fish will naturally take longer than the fillets to cook. You can also cook the fish by bringing 1 litre (1¾ pints) water to the boil with the thyme sprigs and a little seasoning; place the fish in a roasting tin, pour the water over them, cover with foil and either cook in the oven (pre-heated to gas mark 5, 375°F/ 190°C), or gently on the hob.

Leave the fish to drain and cool until you can handle them, then skin them and take all the flesh off the bones, or simply skin the fillets and check that there are no bones. Flake the flesh. Melt the butter over a low heat in a heavy pan; add the fish, more salt and pepper and the cayenne and cover to let the fish absorb the butter. Tip into a decorative pot or bowl that will look attractive on the table and put a sprig of parsley to set in the butter. Keep in the fridge and serve as a light lunch or starter.

INGREDIENTS

PREPARATION TIME
20 minutes
COOKING TIME
15 minutes

2 medium-sized trout or 4 fillets
Salt and freshly ground black pepper
Juice of ½ lemon
2 large sprigs of fresh thyme (lemon thyme if possible)
175 g (6 oz) salted butter
A pinch of cayenne
1 sprig of parsley

SPICED BEEF

— • —

INGREDIENTS

PREPARATION TIME
5 minutes
CURING TIME
8 days
COOKING TIME
2½ hours

2 kg (4½ lb) boned and rolled topside beef
120 g (4½ oz) soft brown sugar
15 g (½ oz) juniper berries
25 g (1 oz) whole allspice
25 g (1 oz) black peppercorns
40 g (1½ oz) coriander seeds
120 g (4½ oz) coarse sea salt
150 ml (5 fl oz) stout or red wine
150 ml (5 fl oz) water

A surprisingly easy recipe, considering the excellence of the end product, which makes a good alternative to ham at Christmas. Unlike most other cured and spiced meats, this is only ever eaten cold – never hot. You can accompany it with Nerine's quicker pickled beetroot on p. 23, or Pen-friend's pickled cabbage on p. 25. It makes delicious sandwiches and any left-overs can be potted according to the recipe for Potted game on p. 92.

Rub the beef all over with the sugar and leave, covered, in the fridge, for 24 hours to soften the meat. Then crush the spices roughly, mix with the salt and rub the beef with a little of this mixture. Return the beef to the fridge and next day repeat the massage with some more of the spice and salt mix. Continue for a further 5 days, by which time the salt mix will have been used up. Pre-heat the oven to gas mark 2, 300°F (150°C). Wipe the spices from the meat and put it into a casserole which just holds it. Add the stout or red wine, and the water and put the lid on. Wrap a large sheet of foil round the entire casserole, folding the edges tightly together so that no steam can escape. Cook in the oven for 2½ hours, by which time the beef will be tender and full of wonderful flavour. Allow it to cool for an hour in its cooking liquid before removing and placing it between 2 plates with a weight on top. To serve, slice thinly.

PICKLED TONGUE

—— • ——

W ith the minimum of effort you can produce this set-piece of a Christmas buffet which will taste far better than anything you can buy. Serve this cold with Cumbrian sauce (p. 31), Spicy damson relish (p. 30) or Plum and rosemary jelly (p. 42). Or hot with Bulldog mustard (p. 107).

Find a plastic box, or a deep bowl, which will hold the tongue comfortably. Mix the salt, sugar and spices together and rub them into the tongue, massaging thoroughly, then cover with a lid of foil and leave in the fridge for about 10–12 days, massaging with the mixture (which will quickly become a liquid) every day.

At the end of the curing time, rinse the tongue in cold water and put it in a large pan with the carrots, onions and celery and the bouquet garni. Bring slowly to the boil, skimming off the froth that rises to the surface, then lower the heat and simmer for about 3½–4 hours, or until the meat is tender – you can also do this in a low oven instead of on top of the stove. As it cooks, choose a cake tin with a removable base, or line a round, deep, straight-sided dish with non-stick baking paper. Lift out the cooked tongue, remove the skin which will come off easily, then replace it to cool in the cooking liquid for about an hour before curling it round to fit in the cake tin or dish, placing a saucer on top and weighing this down with a heavy weight. To serve hot, slice it after removing the skin.

INGREDIENTS

PREPARATION TIME
10 minutes
CURING TIME
10–12 days
COOKING TIME
4 hours

*1 fresh ox tongue
(weighing about
1.4 kg/3 lb)*
175 g (6 oz) coarse sea salt
*175 g (6 oz) soft brown
sugar*
*1 teaspoon black
peppercorns, crushed*
A pinch of ground cloves
*½ teaspoon ground
cinnamon*
1 teaspoon ground mace
3 carrots
1 medium onion
2 celery stalks
1 bouquet garni

SALT PORK

—— • ——

INGREDIENTS

PREPARATION TIME
10 minutes
COOKING TIME
1 ½ hours
WAITING TIME
5 days–1 week

FOR THE BRINE
6 juniper berries
10 black peppercorns
Half a whole nutmeg
6 cloves
1 teaspoon coriander seeds
4 litres (7 pints) water
750 g (1 ½ lb) coarse sea
  salt
350 g (12 oz) brown sugar
1.5 kg (3 lb) boneless belly
  pork, skin removed
1 bouquet garni
2 carrots
2 sticks of celery
1 medium onion, peeled
  and halved

This uses another traditional method of preserving which immerses meat in a liquid brine and doesn't necessitate the daily massage required for 'dry' curing. This is the sort of food that earned early ship–board fare for sailors such a bad name; after months at sea, the meat which came out of a brine tub can't have been all that nice, but eaten after only a few days in brine it is one of the most delicious of meats, and a way of rendering a cheap, fatty joint digestible, succulent and full of flavour. To hold the brine you will need something deep and narrow like a plastic bucket, well washed with boiling water beforehand, and a plate which will fit neatly within the circumference of the bucket, plus a clean weight (see p. 14), to keep the meat beneath the surface.

Serve Salt pork hot on a bed of lentils with a piquant mustard sauce (use the Coarse green pepper mustard on p. 107 and add chopped gherkins and capers and plenty of parsley to it), or cold, thinly sliced, with the Raw apple chutney on p. 20 or the Spiced pears on p. 45.

Crush the spices a little and put them in a spice ball or muslin bag, then add them to the water, salt and sugar in a large pan. Bring slowly to the boil, then boil hard for 5 minutes. Take off the heat and leave the brine to get completely cold. Put the pork into your clean bucket or container and strain the brine over it. Put the plate and its weight on top to keep the meat below the brine and leave the pork, covered in its brine, for 5 days to a week. Then take it out, tie it into a neat bolster with string, put it in a pan with the bouquet garni and some flavouring vegetables, cover with cold water, bring to the boil then lower the heat and simmer gently for 1 ½ hours.

RILLETTES

——— • ———

French potted pork, rich and delicious, is the dish to eat on a picnic beside the Loire, together with the wine of the region and a baguette or two. This might seem a dream, but at least you can create part of it very easily; rillettes are easy and cheap to make and an invaluable stand-by to have on hand for a quick snack – they keep well in the fridge too. Eat with French bread and small pickled gherkins, or with wholemeal toast. The fat from the drained juices is wonderful for frying potatoes.

If you can, ask the butcher to remove the pork rind although it is easy to do it yourself with the aid of a really sharp knife. Then cut the pork into rough cubes. Put it in an ovenproof casserole with the rest of the ingredients and mix everything together thoroughly with your hands. Pre-heat the oven to gas mark ¼, 225°F (110°C). Bring the contents of the casserole to a bubble over a medium heat on top of the stove, then cover with foil then the casserole lid and transfer to the oven and leave overnight. Next day, check that the meat has cooked to a melted softness, then tip it into a colander over a bowl and leave to drain and cool. Remove the herb stalks, if you were using fresh ones, then process the meat in a food processor or blender until it is reduced to a coarse mass. Be careful not to reduce it to a featureless paste. Then pot into clean, dry preserving jars. Lift off the congealed fat from the juices which drained into the bowl and melt it and use this to seal the rillettes, if you like, but they will keep well in the fridge without it.

INGREDIENTS

PREPARATION TIME
10 minutes
COOKING TIME
Overnight

900 g–2 kg (2–2 ¼ lb) boneless belly pork
3–4 large garlic cloves, crushed
1 tablespoon sea salt
A generous sprig of rosemary or *1 teaspoon dried*
A generous sprig of thyme or *1 teaspoon dried*
Freshly ground black pepper
A pinch of ground allspice
150 ml (5 fl oz) water

POTTED GAME

——— • ———

INGREDIENTS

PREPARATION TIME
10–15 minutes

*350–450 g (12 oz–1 lb)
cooked game, all bones
(and any bits of shot)
removed*
*175–225 g (6–8 oz)
softened salted butter*
*1–2 dessertspoonfuls
brandy, dry sherry or
madeira*
1–2 pinches ground allspice
*Salt and freshly ground
black pepper*

Any cooked game is a wonderful subject for potting – that is, mixing with half its weight in soft butter and flavouring with spices. It is a good way of using up left-over scraps and turning them into something worthwhile and delicious. Our Victorian and Edwardian forebears would have tucked into them for breakfast – we enjoy them as snacks and starters and they make excellent picnic food, easily transported and easy to eat. The method I give here is suitable for cold pheasant, hare, venison or pigeon. Serve potted game as a starter with toast and a little Rowan jelly (p. 48) or Cumbrian sauce (p. 31). For a simple picnic, take the jar of paste, sticks of celery and some small brown rolls – nothing could be easier.

Dice the meat and weigh it, then put it in the food processor with half its weight in softened salted butter and process to a smooth paste. To each 225 g (8 oz) meat and 100 g (4 oz) butter, add a dessertspoonful of brandy, dry sherry or madeira, a pinch of ground allspice, a generous grinding of pepper and salt to taste, then process again. Pack into a scrupulously clean and dry jar or presentable bowl. Melt more butter to pour over the top if you like, although a piece of greaseproof paper pressed well down over the surface, followed by a lid of cling film will do quite well.

POTTED HERB CHEESE

—— • ——

A useful stand-by, and excellent for using up bits and pieces of cheese. A proportion of a blue cheese such as Stilton or Shropshire Blue added to this is very good, but don't allow that proportion to be more than a third, or the flavour of the herbs won't predominate. The cream is an optional extra – just. It does add to the charm of the dish. Spread this thickly on a piece of wholemeal toast and grill until brown and bubbling for a perfect Welsh rarebit. Or add it to cheese sauces to give them extra character. It also makes excellent sandwiches. I have suggested summery herbs, but in winter you could use a mixture of sage, thyme and rosemary.

───

Put all the ingredients into a bowl over a pan of gently simmering water and stir until melted and smooth. Pour into a clean and dry bowl or jar and cover when cold. This will keep, in the fridge, for about 3 weeks.

INGREDIENTS

PREPARATION TIME
10 minutes
COOKING TIME
10–15 minutes

---

225 g (8 oz) grated hard cheese
4 tablespoons double cream
3 tablespoons dry sherry
1 level tablespoon each finely chopped fresh parsley, tarragon, chives and chervil, or 1 level teaspoon each of more pungent herbs such as sage and thyme

FLAVOURINGS, SEASONINGS AND SAUCES

The 'seasonings' in this chapter consist of blends of herbs and spices, oils and vinegars that are quick to make, keep well in the store-cupboard, and can make all the difference to everyday cooking – you can make a salad special by adding a few drops of Blackberry vinegar (p. 119), or by using oil infused with the aromatic flavour of rosemary (p. 110).

Although I give some recipes for dried herbs, I think it is agreed that dried herbs are never as good as fresh ones, and of course it is now possible to buy fresh herbs all year round. Nevertheless, if you grow your own it can seem wasteful not to prolong their season by drying – or freezing – them. The shrubby, 'evergreen' herbs – thymes and rosemary and some of the sages, lavender and bay – are the ones that survive the drying process best, retaining their flavour longest. Those which die down in the winter – chives, parsley, tarragon, basil and so on – are really best frozen. In between come those such as the marjorams and savories which dry satisfactorily but don't keep longer than a few months. Commercially freeze-dried herbs are widely available and are better than the ordinary dried version in almost all cases.

Amongst the seasoning recipes I have included several for the kind of 'Household Sauces' which were the home-made forerunners of commercial sauces such as Lea & Perrins and HP. They do have a subtlety and depth of flavour that is particularly delicious to my mind, and you can, of course, vary the seasonings to suit your palate. Mrs Raffald's Gravy Browning on p. 100 is so good that it is amazing it hasn't reappeared in more cookery books.

For these sauces and flavoured oils and vinegars it is possible to use similarly decorative bottles to those I advise using for cordials and liqueurs in the next chapter. Spanish recycled glass bottles are useful for oil as their patterns offer a useful grip. Again, all bottles and jars should be very clean and dry before using.

Keeping times for seasonings may vary – dried herbs keep well only for about three months, vinegars keep for years. Oils go rancid after about six to nine months. All are best stored *cool* and *dry* in the dark.

AROMATIC
HERBACEOUS SEASONING

— • —

The recipe for this blend of dried herbs and spices was given by Charles Elmé Francatelli in his famous book *The Cook's Guide*, published in 1888. I was first attracted by the name – it makes you imagine a border of herbs and flowers on a hot summer afternoon – and when I tried it I found it lived up to that. Here it is, as useful in the modern kitchen as in the Victorian, but in half the amount Francatelli found necessary. If you are buying the herbs, you might prefer the flavour of freeze-dried basil to that of dried. This blend is a wonderful seasoning for lots of things – to add to meat loaves, or Bolognese sauce, or a thick vegetable soup, to braised oxtail or jugged hare. Sprinkle it over a joint of meat before roasting, or add it to the stuffing for a turkey or goose, or mix it with a little oil and honey and use as a barbecue marinade.

━━━

Pre-heat the oven to gas mark ¼, 225°F (110°C). Spread out the grated lemon rind and chopped garlic on a sheet of greaseproof paper, place this on a baking tray and leave overnight in the oven. Next day, when both have dried, mix thoroughly with all the other herbs and spices, crumbling the bay leaves into little pieces so that they blend easily. Store in a clean, dry jar with a screw-cap, in a dark place.

INGREDIENTS

PREPARATION TIME
10 minutes
FILLS APPROX. 6 VERY
SMALL JARS

Finely grated rind of 1 lemon
1 garlic clove, finely chopped
15 g (½ oz) ground nutmeg
15 g (½ oz) ground mace
10 g (¼ oz) ground cloves or 2 pinches
25 g (1 oz) ground black pepper
15 g (½ oz) dried bay leaves
25 g (1 oz) dried basil
40 g (1 ½ oz) dried marjoram
25 g (1 oz) dried savory
40 g (1 ½ oz) dried thyme
10 g (¼ oz) cayenne or 2 pinches

HERB FLAVOURED SALT

— • —

INGREDIENTS

PREPARATION TIME
10 minutes
WAITING TIME
1–2 weeks
FILLS 4 SPICE JARS

225 g (8 oz) fine sea salt
2 tablespoons dried
marjoram (or rosemary,
thyme, or sage)

One of the best ways of preserving the flavour of dried herbs is to add them to a basic seasoning, like sugar (see page 112) or salt. Single herb salts are perhaps the most versatile, and it is a nice idea to give a selection of these as a present – thyme, rosemary, marjoram and sage, for instance. Use the salts for seasoning meat and fish, for adding to salad dressings, for stirring into fromage frais to make a subtle flavoured dip for crudités. Sprinkle unsalted potato crisps with a pinch of rosemary salt to make a more interesting snack, or dust freshly baked cheese straws with a little sage salt – and of course they are wonderful for seasoning pastry or mashed potato.

Put the salt and herbs into a processor or blender and process briefly so that the herbs are finely chopped and blended with the salt. Then pot in clean and scrupulously dried jars. Keep for a week or so before using, and use within a year. Best stored in a dark cupboard.

PRESERVED GARLIC

—— • ——

Those who grow their own garlic know how deliciously mild and sweet it is when eaten soon after harvesting in July and August, and now supermarkets and greengrocers are stocking this freshly harvested garlic with increasing frequency. Blanching it and preserving it in oil lengthens this stage, and gives you garlic in its most useful and least powerfully acrid form for adding to salads, uncooked sauces, dips and so on. Even if you are unable to find garlic this fresh, this is a good method of treating it, but avoid using any which is producing green shoots as then it is only really fit for planting.

Separate the heads of garlic into cloves and rinse them under a cold tap. Simmer them, covered, in salted water for 10 minutes, then tip into a colander to drain and become cool enough for you to be able to slip off the skins. Spread the cloves out on sheets of paper towel as you skin them, to blot up any surplus moisture, then pack them into clean, dry jars and top up with oil. Bang each jar on a hard surface to get rid of any air bubbles. Make sure the garlic is covered with oil, then put on the lids and store in a dark, cool place. These should keep for at least 6 months if kept cool.

INGREDIENTS

PREPARATION TIME
20 minutes
COOKING TIME
10 minutes
FILLS 2 MEDIUM SIZED
JARS

6 heads fresh garlic
Salt
About 300 ml (10 fl oz)
  olive oil, or olive and
  sunflower oil mixed

SPICED CLARIFIED BUTTERS

—— • ——

PREPARATION TIME
10 minutes
INFUSING TIME
10 minutes
FILLS 1 MEDIUM JAR

Clarified butter is very good for frying as the melting and straining process gets rid of the salt (which causes sticking) and other impurities that burn when heated. This recipe spices the butter at the same time, making it even more useful. It will keep for some time in the fridge. Here I give both sweet and savoury versions.

SPICED BUTTER
FOR SWEET DISHES

—— • ——

Use this to fry pancakes, or apple slices for a flan. Also good for making up the pastry for fruit pies.

INGREDIENTS

225 g (8 oz) unsalted butter
1 vanilla pod
10 cm (4 inch) cinnamon stick
½ teaspoon freshly grated nutmeg
A pinch of ground mace
2 cloves

Cut the butter into cubes and put to melt over a low heat, together with the vanilla pod and the spices. When completely melted, put a lid on the pan and leave to infuse for 10 minutes off the heat. Line a sieve with a cloth wrung out in hot water and pour the melted butter through into a clean, dry jar. Leave to get cold, cap and store in the fridge.

SAVOURY
SPICED BUTTER

—— • ——

For stir-frying when you want the flavour of butter rather than oil, for the slow browning of onions for an onion soup, or for braising carrots or other root vegetables.

INGREDIENTS

225 g (8 oz) slightly salted butter
2 garlic cloves, chopped
15 g (½ oz) peeled fresh root ginger, finely chopped
3 crushed cardamon pods
1 teaspoon cumin seeds

Follow the method as for Spiced butter for sweet dishes.

GINGER IN SHERRY

—— • ——

When fresh root ginger was still a new and wonderful thing in England, I was given this tip on how to make the most of any that I managed to buy. Although fresh ginger is available in any good greengrocer or supermarket now, this condiment is so useful that I keep a jar in the fridge anyway. It is a good way to use up the dregs of a bottle of sherry, too. You can use this preserved ginger in all kinds of recipes. It is particularly suitable for many Chinese dishes as the sherry is a good substitute for rice wine. The ginger-flavoured sherry also has a multitude of other uses – use it to mix up some dry English mustard to serve with beef dishes, or add a spoonful to tinned consommé. Add sugar and then cream to it and it makes a most delicious syllabub, or stir it into gingerbread or fruit cakes.

INGREDIENTS

PREPARATION TIME
5–10 minutes
FILLS 1 MEDIUM JAR

100 g (4 oz) fresh root ginger
150 ml (5 fl oz) medium dry sherry

Scrape the skin from the ginger and slice the root into thick pieces. Put these into a clean, dry jar with a good lid, pour the sherry over, adding more if necessary to cover the ginger completely. Bang the jar on a hard surface to get rid of any air bubbles, then cap and leave in a cool place.

MRS RAFFALD'S GRAVY BROWNING

— • —

INGREDIENTS

PREPARATION TIME
10 minutes
COOKING TIME
10–15 minutes
FILLS 1 LARGE OR 2
MEDIUM BOTTLES

600 ml (1 pint) red wine
25 g (1 oz) butter
100 g (4 oz) sugar
15 g (½ oz) allspice
6 cloves
4 shallots, peeled and
*   halved*
2–3 blades mace or ½
*   teaspoon ground mace*
3 dessertspoonfuls
*   mushroom ketchup*
Grated rind of 1 lemon
A generous pinch of salt

A very superior product indeed which bears no comparison to commercial gravy browning – this is something which you should be proud to be seen adding to your gravy. I make it at regular intervals and use it whenever it seems that the sauce or gravy I'm making needs a little extra something. The recipe first appeared in Elizabeth Raffald's *The Experienced English Housekeeper* in 1794, and deserves a revival. The butter rises to the surface once the mixture has cooled and seals out the air, which helps it keep. All the same, store it in the fridge once you have opened the bottle. Add it to the juices in a roasting tin when you are making gravy; use it to deglaze the pan after frying steak, or use it as the base for sauces for game and poultry.

Warm the wine gently over a low heat. In a heavy pan put the butter and sugar to melt over a medium heat; when the mixture begins to froth the sugar has melted and will begin to caramelize – don't let it go black or it will make the flavour bitter. When the mixture is a rich mahogany brown, draw off the heat and slowly and carefully add the warmed wine, stirring all the time. Add the remaining ingredients and return to the heat to simmer gently for 10 minutes. Allow to cool to tepid, then strain and bottle.

DRIED AND FROZEN
HERB BLENDS

—— • ——

Drying home-grown herbs couldn't be easier, as long as you harvest them at the right time; just before they flower, on a dry day and before they have been baked by that day's sun. Tie them into loose bunches and hang them up in a dry place with a good current of air round them. It may look picturesque to hang them in the kitchen, but the reality is that they get covered in greasy dust and steam; it is best to keep an alternative supply for cooking with. When the herbs are thoroughly dry, rub the leaves from the stalks and then store them in small airtight jars or tubs, in a cupboard; a spice rack of clear glass jars looks decorative, but light leaches flavour from the herbs and spices very quickly. Use the same method to harvest herbs which don't dry well, such as parsley and tarragon, chervil and chives, even basil. But instead of drying them, strip the leaves from the stalks, chop finely and freeze in small amounts, well-wrapped in clingfilm. Once you have got your supply of dried or frozen herbs, you can mix them into various blends, ready for use:

ENGLISH BLEND
Equal parts of dried thyme, sage and marjoram – to use in casseroles and stuffings.

ITALIAN BLEND
2 parts oregano to 1 part sage and 1 part basil. For pizza toppings, pasta sauces.

PROVENÇAL BLEND
Equal parts thyme, rosemary, savory and fennel and oregano. For grilled meat and fish.

FINES HERBES
Equal parts of tarragon, chervil, parsley and chives. To freeze, chop the herbs finely and mix together, then place tablespoonfuls on squares of cling film, wrap tightly into small bundles, then store these bundles in a plastic box or thick plastic bag in the freezer. Use a pinch to flavour soups, egg dishes and cream sauces.

HOUSEHOLD SAUCE

—— • ——

INGREDIENTS

PREPARATION TIME
5 minutes
WAITING TIME
2 weeks
FILLS 1 LARGE BOTTLE

*2 garlic cloves, finely
chopped*
*3 tablespoons walnut
ketchup*
*3 tablespoons anchovy
essence*
2 tablespoons soy sauce
1 teaspoon cayenne pepper
*600 ml (1 pint) red wine
vinegar*

This is typical of the kind of sauce that appears in so many Victorian and Edwardian cookery books and is the forerunner of those Brown Sauces still popular today. This is more like a spiced vinegar, which you can treat as a home-made version of Worcestershire sauce, using it to add zest to anything from soup to Welsh rarebit. You can also use it as the basis for a vinaigrette or add it to a barbecue marinade. It is really useful to have around, and is excellent on fish and chips.

——

Into a clean and dry bottle that will hold about 900 ml (1 ½ pints), put the garlic, then add the walnut ketchup, anchovy essence, soy sauce and cayenne. Top it up with the vinegar, cap tightly and shake well once a day for a fortnight, when it will be ready for use. It will keep for many months.

From left to right: BASIL OIL (*page 109*)

SPICED OIL (*page 109*)

HUILE DE PROVENCE (*page 110*)

KING'S OWN SAUCE

—— • ——

Was this the favourite sauce of a king, or did he make it with his own hands or perhaps it was the choice of an entire regiment? The answer is not revealed in the book from which this recipe came, *Pot Luck* by May Byron, published in 1923. I tried it the first summer I had a bumper crop of nasturtiums and liked its pepperiness. Nasturtium flowers are now sold, in summer, as salad ingredients by the better supermarkets and this recipe is a good way of preserving their hot, sweet flavour. A very good dressing can be made using this sauce with olive oil in the proportions of 1 part of King's Own to 6 of oil, a generous pinch of salt and 1 teaspoon of freshly ground green peppercorns. It is especially good with a salad of grilled red peppers, or mixed leaves and flowers.

Fill a clean, dry 600 ml (1 pint) bottle with the nasturtium flowers and the shallot and top up with the vinegar. Leave for 2 months, shaking the bottle from time to time. Strain the vinegar, discarding the flowers and add the cayenne and soy sauce to it and re-bottle.

INGREDIENTS

PREPARATION TIME
5 minutes
WAITING TIME
2 months
FILLS 1 LARGE BOTTLE

A handful of fresh nasturtium flowers
1 shallot, chopped
About 600 ml (1 pint) white wine vinegar
½ teaspoon cayenne
4 tablespoons soy sauce

CRÈME DE CASSIS (*page 122*)

LEMON GERANIUM SYRUP (*page 126*)

FLAVOURED MUSTARDS

—— • ——

Making your own mustard is fun, but it is not a condiment that is particularly quick to do – the seeds need long soaking before grinding or processing, and care should be taken that they don't expand beyond the confines of the container they are soaking in. So in these recipes I cheat and use either dry mustard powder, or ready-mixed varieties, embellished by extra flavourings.

ALLIUM MUSTARD

—— • ——

So called because it draws on three members of the onion family – chives, shallots and garlic. Good for coating steaks before grilling, or stir 2–3 tablespoons into a rabbit stew just before serving.

Work the garlic into a paste with the sugar and then blend all the rest of the ingredients together until well mixed. Leave to stand for an hour before using.

INGREDIENTS

PREPARATION TIME
5–6 minutes
WAITING TIME
1 hour

½ garlic clove
½ teaspoon sugar
1 small jar Dijon mustard
2 teaspoons finely chopped
  fresh chives
1 teaspoon shallot vinegar
  (see p. 117) or red wine
  vinegar and a few drops
  of shallot juice squeezed
  in a garlic press

COARSE GREEN PEPPER MUSTARD

———— • ————

Add a spoonful of this mustard to a cream sauce to serve with salmon, or with chicken.

Mash the drained peppercorns into the mustard, add the crushed fresh bay leaf or dried half and leave for 1 hour before serving.

INGREDIENTS

PREPARATION TIME
5 minutes
WAITING TIME
1 hour

1 tablespoon green peppercorns in brine, drained
6 tablespoons coarse-grain mustard
1 fresh bay leaf or ½ dried, crushed

BULLDOG MUSTARD

———— • ————

The idea for this comes from Eliza Acton, but as this version goes so well with classic English dishes like roast beef, and steak and kidney pie, *and* has such a bite, I called it by a name that seemed more suitable than Mrs Acton's 'Tartar Mustard'.

Mix the mustard powder with the vinegars, add the sugar and leave to blend for an hour before using.

INGREDIENTS

PREPARATION TIME
3 minutes
WAITING TIME
1 hour

2 tablespoons English mustard powder
About 1 teaspoon Chilli and sherry vinegar (see p. 117)
About 1 teaspoon Horseradish vinegar (see p. 118)
A pinch of sugar

FLAVOURED OILS

— • —

Rather like flavoured vinegars at the end of this chapter, it is easy to add your chosen herb or spice to your chosen oil, but there are differences. The first is that oil doesn't keep as long as vinegar, and rancid oil is horrible, whatever it has been flavoured with. So it is best to make up small quantities and use them within a given time – say six months at the outside. The second difference is that the choice of oil is wider and so the matching up can be even more sophisticated.

CHILLI OIL

— • —

INGREDIENTS

PREPARATION TIME
3 minutes
COOKING TIME
10 minutes

6 fresh chillies (3 red and 3 green)
600 ml (1 pint) sunflower oil

I once watched this being made on a vast scale when I visited the production line for a fish dish being made for the store which sells good food as well as good clothes. This is the domestic version and it is good for any spicy casserole or curry, and for frying fish.

Slice the chillies, discarding the seeds, and infuse them in the sunflower oil over a low heat for 10 minutes. Strain the oil and bottle. Keep in a cool, dark place.

BASIL OIL

— • —

This is obviously the oil to drizzle over a tomato salad, but it is also very good to use for the initial sweating of onions for a tomato soup or sauce. Or just pour it, neat, over a plate of warm pasta and inhale the scent before you eat.

Add the leaves from the basil to the bottle of olive oil, together with the salt. Shake well and leave to infuse for a fortnight.

INGREDIENTS

PREPARATION TIME
1 minute
WAITING TIME
2 weeks

A small handful of fresh basil
1 × 250 ml (8 fl oz) bottle of olive oil
A pinch of salt

SPICED OIL

— • —

Perfect for browning onions for curries, for frying potatoes, and for stir-frying chicken or shellfish.

Put the cumin seeds, cardamom pods, fenugreek seeds, coriander seeds and dried red chillies into a thick-based pan over a low heat for about 5 minutes. Crush the spices as they heat, then pour on the groundnut oil and leave over the same low heat for a further 10 minutes. Remove and cool before bottling. You can strain out the spices or not, as you prefer.

INGREDIENTS

PREPARATION TIME
5 minutes
COOKING TIME
15 minutes

1 tablespoon cumin seeds
6 cardamon pods
1 tablespoon fenugreek seeds
2 tablespoons coriander seeds
2 dried red chillies
600 ml (1 pint) groundnut oil

Huile
DE PROVENCE

——— • ———

INGREDIENTS

PREPARATION TIME
3 minutes
WAITING TIME
2 weeks

4 garlic cloves, crushed
A generous sprig of
rosemary
1 teaspoon fennel seeds,
crushed
1 teaspoon dried oregano
1 teaspoon dried thyme
600 ml (1 pint) extra
virgin olive oil from
Provence

Use this to anoint fish or chicken before grilling, baking or barbecuing. An invaluable, versatile oil.

————————

Add all the seasonings to the olive oil. After infusing it for a fortnight you might find it preferable to strain the oil before using.

SALAD DRESSING TO KEEP FOR A LONG TIME

——— • ———

Normally I like to make my salad dressing fresh each time, varying the flavours and ingredients of the dressing to suit the flavours of the salad ingredients. However, if we are off on a self-catering holiday, I don't want to take a doctor's bag of seasonings so I make up a batch of this all-purpose mixture, found in a collection of Edwardian recipes. To make the shallot juice, put a shallot into the garlic squeezer, press hard and the juice that emerges is usually about a teaspoonful – it's not necessary to be very exact here. A teaspoon or two of this dressing added to shop mayonnaise can effect a miracle.

———

Whizz all the ingredients, except the salt and pepper, in a blender or food processor. Taste for seasoning – you may find that you don't need any extra salt or pepper – then decant into a clean jar with an efficient lid. You can use it neat or dilute it with more olive or sunflower oil.

INGREDIENTS

PREPARATION TIME
10 minutes

3 teaspoons shallot juice
1 teaspoon French mustard
*A pinch of English
    mustard powder*
1 teaspoon sugar
*1 teaspoon Worcestershire
    sauce*
*1 scant teaspoon anchovy
    essence*
10 tablespoons olive oil
*1 tablespoon tarragon
    vinegar*
*Salt and freshly ground
    black pepper*

FLAVOURED SUGARS

———— • ————

Flavoured sugars are so useful to have in the cupboard, to make when you have a minute and use when you run out of time to lift a perfectly ordinary dish into something wonderful.

VANILLA SUGAR

One of the best ways of preserving the scent of an expensive vanilla pod is to cut it into short lengths and store it in a jar of sugar. You can use and top up the sugar almost indefinitely, even removing the pod to use it for flavouring jams, before washing and drying it and returning it to the jar. Vanilla sugar has endless uses – sprinkle it on soft fruit, over the top of freshly baked sponge cakes, or use it to flavour custards and sweet sauces.

LEMON SUGAR

Grate the rind of a lemon and mix thoroughly with 450 g (1 lb) caster sugar. Spread on a baking sheet and leave to dry for an hour or so in a very low oven. Tip into a jar and store in a cool dark place. You can make orange sugar in the same way. Try to use unwaxed or organically grown fruit.

ROSE GERANIUM SUGAR

Dry a handful of rose-scented geranium leaves in the airing-cupboard for 48 hours, and then layer them with caster sugar in a large jar. Leave for about a fortnight before using. This is wonderful with soft fruit, or to flavour whipped cream or to make a syrup for a fruit salad. Can be used instead of rose-water to achieve the same effect.

ROSEMARY SUGAR

Add 2 or 3 generous sprigs of rosemary to a jar of sugar. Use to flavour milk puddings, custards, or a plain cake.

LAVENDER SUGAR

Bury half a dozen heads of lavender in a jar of sugar and leave a month before using. Use this to add intriguing flavour to sweet biscuits to serve with fruit sorbets or ice-creams.

*FL*AVOURED TEAS, AND TISANES

—— • ——

You can now buy tea flavoured with anything from apple to chocolate, but to my mind they are almost all overstated, drawing too heavily on 'nature identical' flavourings, rather than the real thing. In fact, nothing could be easier than adding real herb, flower and fruit flavours to good quality tea – the end result is vastly superior to the manufactured kind. And of course you can make up your own mixtures of dried herbs to serve as soothing tisanes. Both teas and tisanes are best drunk without milk.

*T*HREE FLAVOURED TEAS

— • —

REFRESHING SUMMER BLEND
Empty the contents of a 100 g (4 oz) packet of Ceylon leaf tea into a jar with a well-fitting lid. Add a handful of dried lemon balm leaves and half the amount of dried rose-scented geranium leaves. Shake well to mix and store for 2 weeks before drinking.

SPICY WINTER BLEND
Push 6 cloves into the rind from 2 clementines and leave to dry in an airing-cupboard for 24 hours. Then add to 100 g (4 oz) Assam tea, together with a stick of cinnamon, in an airtight container and leave for 2 weeks before drinking.

AROMATIC BLEND FOR COLDS
For this you need green tea, available from health shops and good tea suppliers. Empty the green tea into an air-tight container and add 2 sprigs each of fresh rosemary and thyme, and 2 heads of fresh lavender, and store in a dry place for at least 2 weeks. Inhale the steaming tea before drinking – it really does clear the head.

*T*HREE TISANE BLENDS

——— • ———

SOOTHING EVENING BLEND
Mix equal quantities of dried elderflowers, lemon balm
and camomile. Make as for ordinary tea. The camomile
adds bitterness to this tea and you can add a little honey to
sweeten it if preferred.

DIGESTIVE BLEND
Mix 2 parts dried mint with 1 part dried fennel and 1 part
caraway seed. Drink hot and fairly strong.

FRAGRANT BLEND
Mix equal quantities of dried lime flowers, dried lemon
verbena and dried lavender flowers. Drink hot, or
chilled. (Lemon verbena has a much more pronounced
lemon fragrance than lemon balm, but does need a warm
garden to grow in. It can be bought ready-dried from
herbalists, as can lime flowers.)

*F*LAVOURED VINEGARS

—— • ——

There is no easier or quicker way to preserve the flavour of fresh herbs at their peak than by picking a handful and shoving them into a bottle of vinegar. That is all it takes, basically, but to be really creative the secret lies in matching the right herb with the right vinegar – there's no point in infusing a heavy red wine vinegar with the delicate scent of elderflowers, which blend better with white wine vinegar; on the other hand warm-flavoured basil responds perfectly to a warm-flavoured vinegar such as sherry. Here are a few ideas.

*C*ELERY VINEGAR

—— • ——

There are two methods; either add 40 g (1½ oz) bruised celery seed (make sure you buy this in a food shop, not a seed merchants) to 600 ml (1 pint) white wine or cider vinegar and leave for a month before using. Or, cut 450 g (1 lb) celery into small pieces, put in a preserving jar, sprinkle with 1 teaspoon salt and pour over 600 ml (1 pint) hot white wine or cider vinegar. Allow to cool, cover and leave for a month before straining off the vinegar.

Celery vinegar makes an excellent base for dressings for root vegetable salads such as potato, carrot, beetroot and so on.

ROSEMARY AND BALSAMIC VINEGAR

—— • ——

Into a small bottle of balsamic vinegar (the supermarket version is better for this – the very expensive 'château-bottled' balsamic vinegars are best left alone) push 2 generous sprigs of rosemary. Leave to infuse for at least a month.

This has a warm sweetness which goes wonderfully well with tomatoes.

CHILLI AND SHERRY VINEGAR

—— • ——

Chop 1 red and 1 green chilli into small pieces and add them to a small bottle of sherry vinegar. Leave for a fortnight, then strain and rebottle.

Try adding a teaspoon of this to a beef casserole, or to a robust tomato soup. Also useful in sweet-and-sour dishes.

GARLIC VINEGAR

—— • ——

This is best made when the new crop of garlic has arrived – in late summer – rather than towards the end of its season when it is beginning to develop green shoots. Peel all the cloves from a head of garlic, cut each in half lengthways and put into a clean and dry litre (1¾ pint) bottle. Top up with the vinegar of your choice, or make smaller amounts of different varieties – cider, red or white wine or sherry vinegars. *Shallot vinegar* is made in the same way and is just as useful.

Use for any salad dressing, or add to piquant sauces.

HORSERADISH VINEGAR

— • —

This recipe is straight from Mrs Beeton and is very good. She stresses that this must be made 'either in October or November, as horseradish is then in its highest perfection'. Put 50 g (2 oz) finely chopped or grated horseradish, 15 g (½ oz) finely chopped shallot and a pinch of cayenne into a bottle with 600 ml (1 pint) vinegar. Shake it daily for a fortnight then strain and bottle.

I like this made with cider vinegar, and find it good for potato salads, especially if they accompany cold beef.

ELDERFLOWER VINEGAR

— • —

A lovely delicate vinegar; ideally it should be made with champagne vinegar as the two flavours complement each other well, but you can use white wine vinegar instead. Just shake any insects off 3 heads of elderflowers and push the flowers into the bottle of vinegar. Leave for about 2 weeks before using.

Excellent for fish dishes – try adding a thread of this to a cream sauce for salmon or trout. It also makes a lovely dressing for salads of cooked, mild-flavoured root vegetables, such as salsify and scorzonera, using a light oil such as grapeseed.

RASPBERRY VINEGAR

This became very smart at one stage and you could hardly find a restaurant that didn't make use of it in one way or another. It is so good, however, that it doesn't deserve to disappear because it is no longer new (it is a Victorian invention anyway, as far as I know). Put 450 g (1 lb) raspberries into a lidded container with 600 ml (1 pint) cider vinegar, mashing the fruit a little with a wooden spoon. Leave, covered, for a fortnight. Strain well and put into a pan with 225 g (8 oz) caster sugar for each 600 ml (1 pint) vinegar. Simmer for 10 minutes, cool then bottle.

We have learnt to partner this with calves' liver, *magret* of duck and so on. It makes a good dressing for bitter salad leaves – and our great grandmothers enjoyed it diluted with water as a refreshing drink on a hot day. Other fruit vinegars are made in the same way – blackberry and elderberry are two good ones to try.

CORDIALS, SYRUPS AND LIQUEURS

I n France, bringing out a bottle of your own home-made fruit liqueur is always interpreted as a truly generous gesture of hospitality. It used to be in this country too; many of the recipes I came across for this chapter are Edwardian or Victorian, meant to be prepared by the lady of the house and offered as refreshment at various times of the day, regardless of their alcoholic content. Perhaps one of the reasons that this congenial habit has died is that buying a bottle of spirits isn't a cheap undertaking – it does take a certain nerve to experiment with a bottle of gin or vodka which has cost you almost £10 – so the time to experiment is when you return home with some duty-free. On the plus side, the flavouring ingredients are cheap, or even free, such as elderflowers, or young blackcurrant leaves, or blackberries. They are also very easy to make, although they do take time to mature.

I have included recipes which depend largely on spirits flavoured with other ingredients, and those which contain no alcohol at all, so there should be something to please everyone. Those which are alcoholic are equally delicious when made into more innocent long drinks, topped up with sparkling mineral water.

Most are as useful in cooking as they are pleasant to drink, and they make good presents especially if you use decorative bottles. These can be any that you have carefully saved, or the type made from recycled glass which are fairly widely available. When I am making a non-alcoholic cordial, I wash out the bottles with baby bottle sterilizing fluid to ensure the cordial keeps well.

Use non-alcoholic cordials within six months, but those containing alcohol improve with age and can be kept for several years.

Anisette

— • —

This admirably brief recipe came from *The Complete Indian Housekeeper and Cook*, first published in 1888, and it is an interesting way of improving a bottle of duty-free gin. If you chose to omit the sugar, you will have an aromatic alternative to plain gin-and-tonic, also good topped up with soda rather than tonic and served with a slice of lime. If you prefer to add the sugar, it becomes a good digestive to serve neat at the end of a meal.

Macerate the seeds in the gin for 3 weeks. Add the sugar lumps and leave for a further 3 weeks, shaking the bottle periodically. Then strain and bottle.

INGREDIENTS

PREPARATION TIME
5 minutes
WAITING TIME
6 weeks

1 bottle dry gin
1 dessertspoon aniseed
1 dessertspoon coriander
seeds
1 dessertspoon fennel seeds
6 sugar lumps (optional)

CRÈME DE CASSIS

—— • ——

INGREDIENTS

PREPARATION TIME
30 minutes
COOKING TIME
1 ½ hours
WAITING TIME
2 weeks
FILLS 2 1 LITRE
(1 ¾ PINTS) BOTTLES

*900 g (2 lb) blackcurrants,
stalks removed
1 litre (1 ¾ pints) red wine
900 g (2 lb) sugar
About 750 ml (1 ¼ pints)
brandy*

I make this alcoholic blackcurrant cordial every year for adding to white wine to make a Kir, or to sparkling white wine to make a Kir Royale, as well as to enliven summer pudding, as a flavouring for ice-cream, both bought and home-made, or to give a summery flavour to fruit salads throughout the year. It is a lengthy process but most of the stages take only a few minutes each and it is one of the best ways of capturing that blackcurrant flavour. Follow the same process to make *Crème de mûres* (blackberries), or *de framboises* (raspberries).

Purée the fruit very briefly in a processor or blender, just enough to break it up. Then put it into a glass or china bowl and pour in the wine. Stir well, cover and leave overnight. Next day, tip the contents of the bowl into a jelly bag set over a large, heavy saucepan or preserving pan, and leave it to drip through. Stir in the sugar and set the pan over a low heat and continue to stir until all the sugar has dissolved. Leave the pan, uncovered, on the lowest heat setting so that the contents barely simmer, for about 1½ hours (the idea is to thicken the syrup very slowly without evaporating too much alcohol) and you can do this in the oven on its lowest setting if you prefer. The syrup doesn't need any attention beyond checking that it isn't cooking too fast. Leave to get cold. To get the balance of syrup to brandy right, measure three wine glasses of syrup into a large jug, then add a wineglass of brandy and so on until all the syrup is used up. Stir very well to make sure the brandy and syrup are mixed, pour into clean bottles and cork firmly. Keep for at least a fortnight before using. Best used within a year.

*H*UNZA APRICOT CORDIAL

— • —

Hunza apricots are those small round fruit that look unappetizingly dusty and wrinkled in better health-food stores. They have a wonderful flavour, however, despite or perhaps because of, the fact that they are more stone than fruit. A few spoonfuls of this cordial make a good addition to dried fruit salads, or spooned over a warm *tarte tatin* as it comes from the oven. You can use the left-over apricots, after removing the stones, for desserts such as apricot mousse or for filling crêpes.

Soak the apricots in the white wine overnight, then put both apricots and wine into a heavy pan, bring to a simmer and stir in the honey. Check that the honey has dissolved, then remove from the heat and allow to cool. Return the apricots and their wine and honey syrup to the rinsed-out container in which they spent the night, cover, and leave for 48 hours. Strain into a large jug, add your chosen spirit and stir thoroughly, then pour into clean bottles. Keep for another 2 months before drinking.

INGREDIENTS

PREPARATION TIME
5 minutes plus overnight
WAITING TIME
48 hours plus 2 months

450 g (1 lb) well-washed hunza apricots
1 litre (1 ¾ pints) white wine
275 g (10 oz) clear honey
300 ml (10 fl oz) vodka, rum or brandy

CITRODONE

—— • ——

INGREDIENTS

PREPARATION TIME
15 minutes

*4 large, thin-skinned
lemons (preferably
unwaxed or organically
grown)
550 g (1 ¼ lb) sugar
25 g (1 oz) citric acid
1.2 litres (2 pints) boiling
water*

This name is just another for the simple drink we all know as lemonade – not the fizzy sweet stuff that has been masquerading under the name for years, but the real thing, made with fresh lemons. The recipe I have long used comes from Mrs Hilda Leyel's book *Summer Drinks and Winter Cordials*, published in the 1930s. 'Citrodone' is a name redolent of that era, conjuring up images of tennis parties and motoring picnics. The citric acid helps it to keep all summer long, but you can make a short-term version without it.

———

Wash the lemons well, remove their rind as thinly as possible and squeeze out the juice and put both rind and juice into a large jug, together with the citric acid and sugar. Pour the boiling water over all, stir thoroughly, put a saucer over the jug and leave to cool completely. Strain and bottle and cap tightly. To drink, dilute with mineral water. You can use this as soon as it is cold, or it will keep for at least 3 months.

SHRUB

— • —

This simple and delicious cordial is typical of those concocted by the lady of the house for the delight of her friends. The recipe comes from a North Yorkshire manuscript recipe book compiled in the early years of the last century, translated into modern usage by Peter Brears, director of Leeds City Museums and an expert at such things. He served it at the end of an impressive meal he had cooked from the manuscript recipes – it made an excellent digestive.

Put the spirit and sugar into a bottle and shake until dissolved, then add the orange juice. Cap or cork tightly and shake well once a day for a week. Leave in a cool, dark place until the mixture clears, then strain through a coffee filter paper into a clean bottle.

INGREDIENTS

PREPARATION TIME
10 minutes
WAITING TIME
About 1 month

300 ml (10 fl oz) rum or
brandy
25 g (1 oz) sugar
50 ml (2 fl oz) fresh
orange juice

Flower and leaf syrups

——— • ———

INGREDIENTS

PREPARATION TIME
10 minutes plus overnight

12 heads elderflowers or *a handful of scented leaves*
750 g (1 ½ lb) caster sugar
25 g (1 oz) citric acid (optional)
Rind and juice of 1 lemon
600 ml (1 pint) boiling water

Elderflower syrup is perhaps the best known of the many flower syrups, and it is easy to make at home. You can also make syrups using other flowers and herbs in exactly the same way. Very young blackcurrant leaves have a wonderful aroma of the fruit to come, delicate but distinctive. Rose- or lemon-scented geranium leaves are equally good or try experimenting with any of the mints, with lemon balm, or heavily scented flowers such as pinks or old-fashioned roses; even May blossom was used in old recipes. The addition of citric acid helps the syrup to keep longer, but does add a more pronounced lemony flavour so you can leave it out if you prefer, but then store the syrup in the fridge.

Dilute these syrups to drink at the rate of about 2 teaspoons per tumbler of water. Try a teaspoonful of elderflower syrup in a glass of white wine, topped up with ice-cold sparkling mineral water to make a spritzer, or the same of rose geranium syrup in a glass of rosé wine. They also make wonderful sorbets, or bases for fruit salads. Two tablespoons of elderflower or lemon balm syrup poured over sliced strawberries makes them extra special.

———

Shake the elderflower heads to get rid of any insects or wash the leaves if you feel it to be necessary. Put the caster sugar, citric acid (if using), the thinly pared rind and the juice of the lemon in a large jug and pour the boiling water over all. Then add the elderflowers, or the scented leaves. Stir well, cover and leave to stand overnight. Strain through a coffee filter and bottle, capping tightly.

FRUIT FLAVOURED SPIRITS

— • —

For many years I have been making raspberry brandy, using the simplest and, of their kind, the cheapest ingredients; cooking-quality brandy, raspberries from the garden, a little sugar. The finished product tastes rarified and magical, a shot of the essence of summer. Any fruit will do this for any spirit – a hedgerow will produce enough sloes or elderberries to flavour a bottle of gin, strawberries have a good effect on vodka, damsons render rum much nicer – the method is always the same.

The uses for such flavoured spirits are many and various. Damson or Sloe Gin is a traditional winter drink – try a Damson Gin-and-tonic pick-me-up on Boxing Day morning. Serve the strawberry and raspberry spirits, chilled, with coffee after dinner, or add them to matching desserts to give an added depth of flavour. Cherry Brandy can be added to the gravy to accompany roast duck, or use Plum Whisky to pour round the Christmas pudding.

Prepare the fruit a little – you will need to pierce the tough skins of fruit like damsons or sloes with a needle or skewer, or lightly crush soft fruit. Mix with your chosen alcohol in a large preserving jar, cover and leave for 48 hours, stirring or shaking the contents whenever you remember. Strain through a coffee filter paper, stir in the sugar until it dissolves (you will need a little more than the amount above for sour fruit, a little less for sweet soft fruit such as strawberries), then bottle. Keep for as long as you possibly can before drinking.

INGREDIENTS

PREPARATION TIME
5–10 minutes plus 48 hours plus 10 minutes
WAITING TIME
At least 2 months

About 225 g (8 oz) fruit
1 bottle of spirits
About 100 g (4 oz) sugar

GINGERETTE

— • —

INGREDIENTS

PREPARATION TIME
5 minutes
COOKING TIME
Overnight

15 g (½ oz) cloves
20 g (¾ oz) dried red
chillies
20 g (¾ oz) dried root
ginger, bruised
15 g (½ oz) cinnamon sticks
450 g (1 lb) demerara
sugar
1.2 litres (2 pints) water
5 large juicy oranges
3 large juicy lemons

This is an old family recipe belonging to a friend who describes it as 'a powerful winter warmer', which is something of an understatement. It was published in an earlier book of mine called *The Country Housewife*, which is now out of print and, as I have seen no recipe like it, I felt it was time to give it another airing; it won many fans on its first. I now make it in half quantities since the family is smaller, and infuse the syrup with its powerful amount of spices overnight in a low oven instead of simmering it for an hour on the hob. Drink this diluted with hot water on cold days, after carol singing or on Bonfire Night and there is no better way of chasing a cold. You can add whisky to make a toddy which is hot in all senses.

Pre-heat the oven to gas mark ½, 250°F (120°C). Tie the spices into an old clean handkerchief – a spice ball will be too small to hold this amount – and place them in an ovenproof casserole, together with the sugar and water. Bring to a simmer on top of the stove, check that the sugar has dissolved, cover the casserole and transfer to the oven overnight. Next day, remove the spices and leave the spiced syrup to cool down while you squeeze the juice from the oranges and lemons. Strain the juice into the syrup, mix well and bottle. It will keep some time, but store the opened bottle in the fridge.

SCOTCH CORDIAL

———— • ————

The origin of this powerful liqueur is vague; I was given a recipe for what was known as 'that Scotch drink', but whether it was because the alcohol was Scotch, or because it came from the donor's Scottish grandmother, was never made clear. It is certainly best made with the white currants specified in the recipe as I was given it, but I have cheated and used redcurrants when there were no white ones to be had. Try adding a generous measure of this to fruit cakes. Even better, inject it lavishly into your still-warm Christmas cake while it is still in its baking tin, leave it to cool completely then wrap in cling-film until you want to decorate it.

———

Remove the larger stalks from the currants, then remove the peel from the lemon as thinly as possible. Put the currants, lemon rind, ginger and whisky into a large preserving jar, mix well, cap and leave for a week. Then add the sugar and leave for 2 days, shaking the jar during that time to make sure the sugar dissolves. Strain the cordial twice through a coffee filter paper, then bottle and leave at least 3 months before drinking.

INGREDIENTS

PREPARATION TIME
10 minutes
WAITING TIME
9 days plus 3 months

350 g (12 oz) white currants or *redcurrants*
1 large lemon
1 large piece dried root ginger, bruised
1 bottle blended malt whisky
225 g (8 oz) sugar

VIN DE NOIX

— • —

PREPARATION TIME
10 minutes
WAITING TIME
2 months

12 green walnuts
3 bottles full-bodied red
  wine
450 g (1 lb) sugar
300 ml (10 fl oz) brandy

We were given glasses of this by a master pork butcher who made the best *rillettes* in the Touraine. One evening he invited us to an al fresco meal at his allotment hut – which turned out to be a series of caves boring far back into the hillside above Loches – and from the innermost cave he bore dusty bottles of his pride and joy, made from the walnuts gathered from the tree that shaded the terrace outside. It's powerful stuff. The walnuts should be picked in mid-July, before the shells have begun to harden, or buy them from greengrocers.

—————

Wearing rubber gloves to prevent your hands from staining, cut the walnuts into quarters, or even eighths if you have the patience and put them into a large jar or container with all the other ingredients; an old sweet jar is ideal. Leave, tightly covered, for 2 months, shaking or stirring it twice a week. Strain it carefully and bottle it, and keep for New Year (the traditional time to drink it).

POMANDER RATAFIA

— • —

The Victorians were very fond of making ratafias, which are by definition a concoction of fruit flavoured spirits to which a sugar syrup is added. They are powerfully alcoholic, so don't be fooled by their innocently sweet and fruity flavours. This recipe is a variation of orange ratafia, one of the most popular, and makes a decorative present. You could claim that this ratafia was a powerful remedy for a cold, with its orange and clove content – try it half and half with hot water. A spoonful or two also makes a good addition to a dried fruit salad.

Scrub the orange well in hot water, or use an unwaxed orange. Stick the cloves all over it as though you were making a pomander ball, then put it in a large preserving jar and pour the vodka over it. Make up a syrup with the water and sugar and simmer for 10 minutes. Allow to cool, then add the orange flower water and add to the vodka in the jar. Clip or screw on the lid and leave for at least 3 months, shaking the jar from time to time, then strain off the ratafia into clean bottles. If giving it as a present, don't remove the orange as it looks interesting and attractive; place it in a clean jar and strain the ratafia over it.

INGREDIENTS

PREPARATION TIME
15–20 minutes
COOKING TIME
10 minutes
WAITING TIME
3 months

1 small juicy orange
15 g (½ oz) cloves
1 bottle vodka
300 ml (10 fl oz) water
175 g (6 oz) sugar
1 tablespoon orange flower
water

HOP AND SHERRY TONIC

——— • ———

INGREDIENTS

PREPARATION TIME
1 minute
WAITING TIME
1 month

---

1 bottle dry or medium dry sherry
A small handful of dried hops (weighing about 40–50 g/1 ½–2 oz)
175 g (6 oz) sugar (optional)
300 ml (10 fl oz) water (optional)

This was much recommended to Victorian ladies who were suffering from nervous exhaustion (which must have been much the same as our modern malady, stress) – the hops to soothe and calm, the sherry to cheer. You can make this without the syrup, in which case the result is an aromatically bitter vermouth-like apéritif which is also good for cooking (try adding a few tablespoons to a sauce for fish) but the syrup adds sweetness for those who prefer it. (Although it will take a little longer to prepare and you will have to wait 2 months before drinking the tonic.) You can buy small amounts of hops from any shop that supplies home beer-makers. You can serve the unsweetened version of this tonic as a long drink topped up with soda, ice and a slice of lemon or orange, or short over ice. The sweetened version makes a good 'unwinding' drink at the end of a long working day, again short or long, or even topped up with hot water on a cold evening.

———

Pour the contents of the sherry bottle over the hops in a preserving jar, cover tightly and leave for a month, shaking the jar from time to time. If you would like to sweeten the drink, make up a syrup by dissolving the sugar into the water over a low heat, bring to the boil, boil for 10 minutes and allow to cool completely. Add this syrup to the sherry strained of its hops, and bottle. Wait another month before drinking. If you prefer not to sweeten it, simply strain out the hops and bottle the liquid – you can drink it at once.

INDEX

Page numbers in *italic* refer to colour photographs

A

Anchovies	15
Anisette	121
Apples	
and Mint Relish	21
Raw Apple Chutney	20
Spiced Apple Honey	51
Apricots	
Dried Apricot and Lemon Jam	50
Hunza Apricot Cordial	123
Peach and Apricot Preserve	66
Aromatic Herbaceous Seasoning	95

B

Beef, Spiced	88
Beetroot, Nerine's Quicker	
Pickled	23, *33*
Blackberries	
Crème de Mures	122
Quick Bramble Jam	54, *67*
Vinegar	94
Blackcurrants	
Crème de Cassis	*104*, 122
Blackcurrant and Geranium	
Jelly	52
Blackcurrant Leaf Syrup	126
Blackcurrant Mincemeat	55
Summer Berry Jam	53
Boil, full rolling	19
Bottles	
sizes	8
decorative	13, 120
Brandy	
Cherry	127
Kumquats in Brandy Syrup	63, *67*
Raspberry	127
Bread and Butter Pickles	22
Brine	90
containers	14
Butter	
clarified	79
spiced	98

C

Cabbage, Pen-friend's Pickled	25
Candied Peel, Honey	73
Cheese	
Damson	57
Goat's, in Oil	24
Potted Herb	*70*, 93
Cherries	
in Wine	59
Quick Spiced	27
Chutney	
Chinoiserie (kiwi fruit)	26
Courgette	28
Raw Apple	20
Citrodone (lemonade)	124
Cod's Roe Paste	80
Cordials	120
Hunza Apricot	123
Scotch Cordial	129
Corn Relish	29, *33*
Courgettes, Chutney	28
Crème de Cassis	122
Cumbrian Sauce	31
Curd	
Lime	60
Seville Orange	60

D

Damsons	
Cheese	57
Gin	127
Spicy Damson Relish	30
Damson and Walnut Jam	56

E

Eggs	
Pickled	32
Quail	32

Elderberry	
Gin	127
Vinegar	119
Elderflower	
Syrup	126
Vinegar	118

F

Flowers	
Crystallised	58
Syrups	126
Food mill	12
Freezer jams	61

G

Game, Potted	92
Garlic	
Fierce Garlic Paste	35
Preserved	97
Vinegar	117
Geraniums	
Blackcurrant and Geranium	
Jelly	52
Lemon Geranium Syrup	*104*, 126
Rose Geranium Sugar	112
Rose Geranium Syrup	126
Ginger	
freeze dried	17
in Sherry	99
Gingerette	128
Rhubarb, Orange and Ginger	
Jam	77
Gooseberries	
Eliza Acton's Groseillée	62
Gravlax, Karin Perry's	81
Gravy Browning, Mrs Raffald's	100
Greek Rarebit	24

H

Haddock
  Smoked Haddock Paste   84
Herbs
  Aromatic Herbaceous
    Seasoning   95
  Blends   101
  dried   101
  Herb Flavoured Salt   96
  fresh   94
  frozen   101
  Herbes de Provence   15
  jellies   41
  Potted Herb Cheese   70, 93
Herrings, Rollmop   82
  and see Soused Mackerel   83
Honey
  Honey Candied Peel   73
  Spiced Apple   51
Hop and Sherry Tonic   132
Horseradish vinegar   118

J

Jam funnel   14
Jams
  Damson and Walnut   56
  Dried Apricot and Lemon   50
  Eliza Acton's Groseillée   62
  Freezer   61
  Quick Bramble   54, 67
  Rhubarb, Orange and Ginger   77
  Summer Berry   53
  Superfine Raspberry   74
  Tomato   78
Jars   13
  sizes   8
  warming, importance of   10
Jellies
  Blackcurrant and Geranium   52
  herb flavoured   41
  Orange and Thyme   39
  Plum and Rosemary   34, 42
  Rowan   31, 48
  Seville Orange   64
Jelly bag and stand   13

K

Kiwi Fruit
  Chinoiserie Chutney   26
Kumquats in Brandy Syrup   63, 67

L

Leaves, Scented
  Crystallised   58
  in Syrups   126
  in Teas and Tisanes   114–5

Lemons
  Citrodone (lemonade)   124
  Dried Apricot and Lemon Jam   50
  Lemon Sugar   112
  Preserved Lemons and
    Olives   34, 36
Lemonade see Citrodone   124
Lids   13
Limes   60
  Lime Curd   60
  Salmon Cured in Vodka and
    Lime   69, 85

M

Mackerel, Soused   83
Marmalade, Ruby Orange   71
  and see Seville Orange Jelly   64
Mincemeat, Blackcurrant   55
Mint
  Apple and Mint Relish   21
  Syrup   126
Mulberries
  in Freezer Jams   61
Mushrooms, Exotic, in Oil   37
Mustard
  Allium   106
  Bulldog   107
  Coarse Green Pepper   107
  Dijon   16
  English   16
  seed   16

N

Nectarines, Preserved   65, 68

O

Oils
  Basil   103, 109
  Chilli   108
  Exotic Mushrooms in Oil   37
  flavoured   19
  Goat's Cheese in Oil   24
  Huile de Provence   103, 110
  rosemary   94
  Spiced   103, 109
  storage   11, 94
  varieties   16, 19
Olives   16
  Cassées   38
  Preserved Lemons and
    Olives   34, 36
Onions, Sweet and Sour   40

Orange
  flower water   16
  Orange and Thyme Jelly   39
  Pomander Ratafia   131
  Rhubarb, Orange and Ginger
    Jam   77
  Ruby Orange Marmalade   71
  Seville orange curd   60
  Seville Orange Jelly   64
  Shrub (orange cordial)   125

P

Pastes
  Cod's Roe   80
  Fierce Garlic   35
  Smoked Haddock   84
Peach and Apricot Preserve   66
Pears, Spiced   45
Pectin
  content in fruit   9
  sugar   17
Pepper, Red, and Tomato
  Preserve   41
Peppercorns
  Coarse Green Pepper Mustard   107
Pickles
  Bread and Butter Pickle   22
  Mrs Beeton's Excellent Pickle   43
Pickled
  Beetroot   23
  Cabbage   25
  Eggs   32
  Tongue   89
Pineapple Relish   44
Plums
  Plum and Rosemary Jelly   34, 42
  plum whisky   127
Pomander Ratafia   131
Pork
  Rillettes (French potted pork)   91
  Salt   90
Postal Suppliers   14, 18, 136
Potted
  Game   92
  Herb Cheese   70, 93
  Shrimps   86
  Trout   87
Preserved
  Garlic   97
  Lemons and Olives   34, 36
  Nectarines   65, 68
Preserves
  Apulian Tomato   46
  Peach and Apricot   66
  Red Pepper and Tomato   41
  Strawberry and Redcurrant   68, 76
Preserving Pans   12
Pressure Cooker   12, 64
Prunes, Fragrant   72

R

Raisins, Christmas 75
Raspberries
  Raspberry Brandy 127
  crème de framboises 122
  Eliza Acton's Groseillée 62
  Freezer Jam 61
  Summer Berry Jam 53
  Superfine Raspberry Jam 74
  Vinegar 119
Redcurrants
  Scotch Cordial 129
  Strawberry and Redcurrant
    Preserve *68*, 76
Relish
  Apple and Mint 21
  Corn 29, *33*
  Pineapple 44
  Spicy Damson 30
Rhubarb, Orange and Ginger
  Jam 77
Rillettes (French potted pork) 91
Rollmop Herrings 82
Roses
  Crystallised 58
  Rose Geranium Sugar 112
  rose water 16
Rosemary
  oil 94
  Plum and Rosemary Jelly *34*, 42
  Sugar 112
  Vinegar, Balsamic 117
Rowan Jelly 48

S

Salad Dressing
  To Keep a Long Time 111
Salmon
  Cured in Vodka and Lime *69*, 85
  Karin Perry's Gravlax 81
Salt
  Herb Flavoured 96
  Pork 90
  types 16
Saltpetre 79
Sauces
  Cumbrian 31
  Household 102
  King's Own 105
Setting Point 10

Sherry
  Ginger in Sherry 99
  Hop and Sherry Tonic 132
  Vinegar, Chilli and 117
Shrimps, Potted 86
Shrub (orange cordial) 125
Sloe gin 127
Smoked Haddock Paste 84
Soused Mackerel 83
Spiced
  Apple Honey 51
  Beef 88
  Butters 98
  Oil *103*, 109
  Pears 45
Spices
  Aromatic Herbaceous
    Seasoning 95
  spice ball 13
  varieties 17
Spirits, fruit flavoured 127
Storage
  jams and jellies 10
  oils 11, 94
  potted meat and fish 11, 79
  vinegars 11, 94
Strawberries
  Freezer Jam 61
  Strawberry and Redcurrant
    Preserve *68*, 76
Sugar
  dissolving carefully 9
  Lavender 112
  Lemon 112
  Rose Geranium 112
  Rosemary 112
  Vanilla 112
  types 17
Syrups
  Brandy, Kumquats in 67
  Flower and Leaf 126
  Lemon Geranium *104*, 126
  Rose Geranium 126

T

Tabasco 17
Tapénade with Dried Tomatoes 47
Teas 113–4
  Aromatic, for Colds 114
  Refreshing Summer 114
  Spicy Winter 114

Thyme
  Orange and Thyme Jelly 39
  in herb blends 95, 96, 101
Tisanes
  Digestive 115
  Fragrant 115
  Soothing Evening 115
Tomatoes
  Apulian Tomato Preserve 46
  dried 17
  Red Pepper and Tomato
    Preserve 41
  Tapénade with Dried
    Tomatoes 47
  tinned 17
  Tomato Jam 78
Tongue, Pickled 89
Trout, Potted 87

V

Vanilla
  types 18
  Sugar 112
Vin de noix 130
Vinegar
  Balsamic, and Rosemary 117
  Blackberry 119
  Celery 116
  Elderberry 119
  Elderflower 118
  Garlic 117
  Horseradish 118
  Raspberry 119
  Sherry, and Chilli 117
  storage 11, 19
  varieties 18, 19
Vodka
  Salmon Cured in Vodka and
    Lime *69*, 85
  strawberry flavoured 127

W

Walnuts
  Damson and Walnut Jam 56
  Vin de Noix 130
Wine
  Cherries in Wine 59
  Vin de Noix 130

Useful equipment (see pages 12 to 14)
and vanilla extract are available from

LAKELAND PLASTICS LTD
Alexandra Buildings
Windermere
Cumbria LA23 1BQ
Tel: 0539488100

A wide range of herbs,
spices and flavours is available from

FOX'S SPICES LTD
Aston Cantlow Road
Wilmcote
Stratford-upon-Avon
Warwickshire
CV37 9XN
Tel: 0789 266420